AF600156

THE CATHOLIC UNIVERSITY OF AMERICA
CANON LAW STUDIES
No. 114

THE CANONICAL ERECTION OF PARISHES

AN HISTORICAL SYNOPSIS AND COMMENTARY

A DISSERTATION

Submitted to the Faculty of Canon Law of the Catholic University of America in Partial Fulfillment of the Requirements for the Degree of

DOCTOR OF CANON LAW

BY

REV. NICHOLAS P. CONNOLLY, J.C.L.
Priest of the Archdiocese of San Francisco

THE CATHOLIC UNIVERSITY OF AMERICA
1938

NIHIL OBSTAT:

EDUARDUS ROELKER, S.T.D., J.C.D.,
Censor Deputatus.

Washingtonii, die XVIII Maii, 1938.

IMPRIMATUR:

✠ JOANNES J. MITTY, D.D.,
Archiepiscopus Sancti Francisci.

die XVIII Maii, 1938.

PRINTED IN THE UNITED STATES OF AMERICA
BY THE WATKINS PRINTING CO., BALTIMORE

TO MY MOTHER AND FATHER

TABLE OF CONTENTS

FOREWORD

In presenting an outline of the history of the development of the parochial system in the Church one is faced with lack of evidence that Christ, the divine Founder of the Church, left His new Society with any detailed plan of internal territorial organization. Aside from the possibility that St. Peter may have been given Rome as his own particular headquarters,[1] and aside from the general mission given to the Apostles to teach all nations,[2] it cannot be convincingly argued that there were any specific rules obliging the individual Apostles to subdivide their territory according to a predetermined plan. Even those few authors who held that the office of pastor was of divine institution did not go so far as to say that parishes with definite boundaries were divinely prescribed.[3]

The government of the faithful throughout all times has therefore been accomplished in whatever way has appeared to be best adapted to the actual circumstances of the age, subject of course to the divinely established constitution of the Church. The constitution concerns itself with the perpetuation of the essential hierarchical character of the Church as Christ left it. That parish organization is not part of that essential character is a conclusion in harmony with the meager available historical data.[4]

A synopsis of the history of legislation on parishes necessarily consists chiefly of the history of the parish institute itself which chronologically precedes the legislation.

The second part of the present work interprets the law as it

[1] Tanquery, *Synopsis Theologiae Dogmaticae,* I, 479, Paris: Desclée et Socii, 1927.

[2] Matthew, XXVIII, 18, 19.

[3] For discussion, see Gonzales, *Commentarium in Decretales,* lib. III, tit. 29, n. 10; Bouix, *De Parocho,* p. 43; Wernz, *Ius Decretalium,* II, n. 821.

[4] Bouix, *De Parocho,* p. 43; Coronata, *Institutiones Iuris Canonici,* I, n. 304; Wernz, *Ius Decretalium,* II, n. 821.

exists today. Parish organization is now obligatory in so far as possible in all territory of the Latin Church. The general law of the Church is so comprehensive in scope as to be uniformly applicable in practically the whole Western Church; yet at the same time it is admirably sufficient, without supplementary particular legislation, normally to supply the needs of local diocesan organization under widely different circumstances.

The welfare of souls has been the primary factor in developing the present general law on the erection of parishes: it is also the chief consideration to guide the ordinary amidst many perplexing problems in the application of that law.

With pleasure the author acknowledges his profound gratitude to His Excellency, the Most Reverend John J. Mitty, Archbishop of San Francisco, for the opportunity to pursue advanced studies. He is also genuinely grateful for the help, suggestions, and guidance so generously offered by the members of the Faculty of the School of Canon Law at the Catholic University.

CHAPTER I

PRELIMINARY NOTIONS

ART. 1. ORIGIN AND DEFINITION OF TERM

ORIGIN OF TERM

The word *paroecia,* found in the Code of Canon Law, is probably derived from the Greek *παροικίας* (*παροικέω*; to live near), and it originally signified a place of habitation, a territory.[1] The Bible uses various derivatives of the verb in the literal Greek meaning of "sojourning" and "sojourner".[2] In time the word came to be used mystically in the sense of "sojourning" in the world where the converts have not "an abiding city".[3]

From that symbolic meaning it is easy to see that the Christians would be quick to adopt the name "sojourners" for themselves. In fact, the Church of Rome describes itself as "the sojourning Church of God", as does also the Church of Smyrna.[4] Further-

[1] Rossi, *De Paroecia,* p. 1.

[2] In the Septuagint, in *Exodus,* II, 22; *Deut.,* V, 14; *II Kings,* VIII, 1. In the New Testament it has this same sense in *Acts,* VII, 29; *Ephes.,* II, 19; *Hebr.,* XI, 9.

[3] *I Pet.* I, 17; Clement of Rome, *II Epist. ad Corinth.,* cap. 5—Rouet de Journel, *Enchiridion Patristicum,* n. 102; MPG, I, 336. This *II Epistle to the Corinthians* is first mentioned by Eusebius (*H.E.,* III, 37) who considered it spurious. It is contained in the Codex Alexandrinus. It is nowadays considered spurious, but very ancient. See Lightfoot, *Apostolic Fathers,* part I, vol. II, 191-208.

[4] St. Clement of Rome, *I Epist. ad Corinth.,* c. 1—Lightfoot, *Apostolic Fathers,* part I, vol. II, 5; St. Polycarp, *Epist. ad Philipp.,* inscription —Lightfoot, *op. cit.,* part II, vol. III, 321.

[5] See Inscription of Encyclical letter which the Church of Smyrna sent to the neighboring church regarding the martyrdom of its bishop, St. Polycarp: "Ecclesia Dei quae Smyrnae peregrinatur (*ἐκκλησία . . . ἡ παροικοῦσα Σμύρναν*), Ecclesiae Dei quae Philomelii peregrinatur, et omnibus ubique terrarum sanctae et Catholicae Ecclesiae paroeciis, misericordia, pax, etc. . . ."—MPG, V, 1029; Journel, *Enchiridion Patristicum,* n. 77.

more, about the year 156 the Church of Smyrna addressed itself to the " 'parishes' of the Catholic Church throughout the world." [5] In this sense *paroecia* would signify the whole city with its environs under its own bishop or metropolitan.

If the original Greek had lent itself only to the meaning just outlined, it would have spared historians the lasting confusion born of ambiguous terminology, because it would then have continued to mean a diocese exclusively. But etymologically, it also meant "neighbor" or those "dwelling near a city". When small groups of Christians in the rural districts beyond easy traveling distance of the city churches began to gather in convenient places, what more natural name could be given their congregation than that of "parish"?

Unfortunately for the historian, the early Christians used the one word quite indiscriminately to designate either whole ecclesiastical colonies with the bishop at the head,[6] or subdivisions of the bishop's territory corresponding more nearly to our parishes.[7] On the other hand, some councils use the word "diocese" for parish.[8] Only about the time of the Council of Trent (1545-63) did this confusion disappear.[9] Since the Code uses the word

[6] A few leading instances are the Council of Ancyra (314), can. 18—Harduin, I, 278; *Apostolic Constitutions,* II, 1, and VIII, 10—MPG, I, 594 and 1086; III Council of Toledo (589), cap. 20—Mansi, IX, 998; Council of Merida (666), can. 19—Mansi, XI, 85; Carolingian Capitularies, e.g., Karlomanni Capit. (742), can. 3—Mansi XVII B, *147; and many others. This use even seems to have been so common that it was employed in opposition to "province" by St. Boniface of Mayence, *Ep. 49 ad Zachariam* (742): "tres ordinavimus episcopos in provinciam et tres parochias decrevimus."—MPL, LXXXIX, 741. See IV Lateran Council (1215), cap. 3—Mansi, XXII, 990.

[7] *Apostolic Constitutions,* II, 58—MPG, I, 737; Council of Nicea (325), can. 16—Harduin, I, 330; Council of Chalcedon (451), can. 17—Harduin, II, 608; *Canons of the Apostles,* 14—Harduin, I, 14; Council of Agde (506), can. 21—Mansi, VIII, 328; Hincmar of Reims, in Capit. Synod., tit. 5, can. 1—MPL, CXXV, 795.

[8] Council of Agde (506), can. 54—Mansi, VIII, 334; Harduin, II, 1004; Council of Tarragona (516), can. 8—Mansi, VIII, 542; Harduin, II, 1042; IV Council of Toledo (633), can. 36—Mansi, X, 629.

[9] Coronata, *Institutiones Iuris Canonici,* I, 351, footnote.

paroecia exclusively, although the sources also use the spelling *parochia* indiscriminately, the distinction between the two is of only speculative importance nowadays.

DEFINITION OF TERM

Canon 216, § 1. Territorium cuiuslibet dioecesis dividatur in distinctas partes territoriales; unicuique autem parti sua peculiaris ecclesia cum populo determinato est assignanda, suusque peculiaris rector, tanquam proprius eiusdem pastor, est praeficiendus pro necessaria animarum cura.

§ 2. Pari modo vicariatus apostolicus et praefectura apostolica, ubi commode fieri possit, dividantur.

§ 3. Partes dioecesis de quibus in § 1, sunt *paroeciae;* partes vicariatus apostolici ac praefecturae apostolicae, si peculiaris rector eisdem fuerit assignatus, appellantur *quasi-paroeciae*.

§ 4. Non possunt sine speciali apostolico indulto constitui paroeciae pro diversitate sermonis seu nationis fidelium in eadem civitate vel territorio degentium, nec paroeciae mere familares aut personales; ad constitutas autem quod attinet, nihil innovandum, inconsulta Apostolica Sede.

The Code does not directly define the word "parish", but from the elements listed in canon 216 it is possible to arrive at a satisfactory notion of what is meant thereby. The constitutive elements of a parish are these: a community of the faithful; a definite territory or, by exception, a definite and exclusive classification or group of persons distinguished from other persons by certain personal characteristics; a priest with rights and duties involving the care of souls among the faithful in the Christian community; and a parish church. It is also necessary that the parish be canonically established as such.

The community of the faithful is composed of those who are baptized. By baptism a person is made a member of the Catholic Church, and becomes capable of enjoying the rights and becomes bound to fulfil the duties that flow from membership in the Church, unless by reason of some defect he is deprived of some of his rights. Consequently non-Catholics, because they are not allowed to communicate in divine worship with Catholics, are for practical considerations excluded from membership in the parish. On the other hand the Code in canon 1350 recommends them to the zeal of the pastor.

The parochial community of the faithful is the ultimate subdivision of a larger ecclesiastical organization, namely, the diocese. The fact that it is a distinct subdivision of a diocese implies that each parish is to be limited by clearly defined boundaries in such a way that there is neither overlapping nor obscurity of limits. It is not correct to restrict the term "canonical parish" to those that are separated from one another on a territorial basis because, while normally the limits are territorial, they may also be determined by other characteristics such as nationality, language, personal qualities, or family privileges. No matter what the actual basis is for the distinction it suffices that there be some norm which restricts the membership to a certain definite congregation of baptized Catholics.

Membership in the particular Christian community or group is determined in the case of strictly territorial parishes by the place of domicile or quasi-domicile, which is regulated by the prescriptions of canons 92-95. Membership in national and other non-territorial parishes is regulated by the possession of certain personal characteristics or acquired privileges. Although the latter type of parishes is legally recognized as canonical it is of a nature so exceptional that the Holy See reserves to itself the exclusive right to establish or to change any of them.

Another element comprised in the notion of a parish is the rector who, as pastor, is to exercise the care of souls therein. Actually, however, a parish can exist without a pastor. It would be more accurate to say therefore that the constitutive element in this case is the pastoral office without which there can be no parish. The pastoral office is permanent, and continues to exist even during intervals when no priest is assigned to exercise it.

Finally, there must be a parish church. While this is not strictly speaking a constitutive element, it is prescribed by law in every case, and it is so necessary that without it the conduct of parish functions is excessively restricted and impaired. Although oftentimes the church has not yet been built when the parish is canonically established, nevertheless it is usually comprised in the notion of a fully organized parish.

A parish is not a community of persons. Indeed, the Christian community is but one of the constitutive elements of a parish. It is not enough that all the essential elements be realized. They must be canonically erected into a parish by the act of a competent superior before they can be considered a parochial unit.

Art. 2. Forms of Parochial Organization

The adaptability of the institution known as parishes is such that it can supply the needs of people in every part of the world in practically all circumstances without losing its identity. The variations are numerous.

TERRITORIAL FORMS

The division along territorial lines has been found to be most feasible as well as most natural and obvious. It is based on the custom of most peoples to live a stable life within more or less easy traveling distance of a common convenient meeting place. It is quite commonly accepted in human society that for the sake of government separate communities should be assigned to local officers, and that these communities be separated by territorial limits from adjoining communities. It is quite natural, therefore, that for the sake of more effective government the Church should divide her numerous diocesan flocks into separate communities, each with its own definite territory, and that in the position of authority over each distinct group she should place a pastor. Complete territorial division is mandatory, in so far as is possible, in every diocese and in every vicariate or prefecture apostolic.

If the prescripts of canon 216, § 1, are fulfilled in reference to a given part or section of a diocese, that part is, according to § 3 of the same canon, a parish. The same is true of territorially independent abbacies and prelacies, whose territory may be divided into parishes.[10] Even though the diocese is one which was subject to the Congregation of the Propaganda until the issuance of the constitution *"Sapienti consilio"*, of June 29, 1908, or which still remains subject to that Congregation, nevertheless the partitions which fulfil the requirements of § 1 are parishes.[11] Similarly any corresponding part of a prefecture or vicariate apostolic in missionary countries subject to the Congregation of the Propaganda is known as a *quasi-parish,* although the name *mission* may be used.[12]

The Code, by using one and the same list of essential characteristics to describe both parishes and quasi-parishes, implies that fundamentally they are identical institutions. The distinction between them depends upon the status of the hierarchical unit of which they are part, and upon certain juridical effects touching the incumbent priest. They differ, for example, in regard to the stability of the pastor in office,[13] in regard to the nomination of a pastor,[14] and in regard to the frequency with which the priest holding the office of rector or pastor must offer mass for the people. Except where explicit ruling is made to the contrary, quasi-pastors are by law equivalent to pastors in regard to parochial rights and obligations as described in canons 461-470.[15]

Filial or subsidiary churches, also known as chapels, are subordinate churches which are not parish churches, even though they may have a certain territory assigned to them and may be in charge of an assistant priest.[16] They exist within the boundaries of the parish on which they are dependent, and the parishioners belong to the whole parish, not merely to that chapel.[17] They are permitted when the very small or fluctuating

[10] Cf. canons 215, § 2 and 319, §§ 1 and 2.

[11] S. C. Prop. Fid., decr., Dec. 9, 1920—AAS, XIII (1921), 17-18.

[12] Can. 216, § 2; S. C. Consist., declar., Aug. 1, 1919, n. 1—AAS, XI (1919), 346.

[13] Can. 454, § 4.

[14] Can. 457.

[15] Can. 451, § 2.

[16] Can. 476, § 2; Ayrinhac, *Constitution of the Church,* p. 304.

[17] S. C. C., *Wrastilavien,* July 13, 1918—AAS, XI (1919), 46-51, esp. p. 49.

number of the people or the absolute lack of a suitable source of income makes the erection of an independent parish inadvisable.[18]

In the prefectures or vicariates apostolic in missionary countries, where it has been found impractical or impossible to maintain a quasi-parish or to supply a sufficient number of priests for the normal spiritual ministry in a very large district, it is sometimes advisable to establish *stations,* that is, to make territorial divisions, assigning to each a particular church or oratory but no particular rector, or one removable at the will of the ordinary, in order that traveling missionaries may minister to the people at central locations at more or less regular intervals.[19]

More or less closely resembling the normal territorial parish is the permanent vicarage, a form of parochial organization that is enveloped in considerable obscurity on account of the scant attention it receives in the common law. Canon 1427 which is the only canon that explicitly mentions it, does not describe it. Reference is made elsewhere to permanent vicars of various kinds, but without casting much light on the problem at hand. There is to be found an implicit reference to permanent vicarages in canon 1412, 1°, where, by excluding from the classification of benefice "parochial vicarages that are not permanently established", the law implies that permanent vicarages can be benefices.

The term *permanent vicarage* is elastic enough to include several different types of parochial organizations which are found both under the former and the present discipline. Pirhing and Schmalzgrueber describe one type. After dividing a parish, instead of founding a new parish the local ordinary might assign the territorial parochial rights in the new district to a succursal church or chapel which, though permanently divided from the mother church, is not fully independent of it. The pastor of the principal church retains primary, or radical jurisdiction over the people belonging to the chapel, but he loses the right to exercise it. His jurisdiction is, as it were, suspended. Complete actual care

[18] S. C. Consist., Aug. 1, 1919, nn. 3 and 8—AAS, XI (1919), 346.

[19] Maroto, *Institutiones,* II, n. 771, II. S.C.C., *Wrastilavien.,* Jul. 13, 1918—AAS, XI (1919), 50.

and administration in spiritual and temporal matters is confided permanently to the vicar by a sort of participation in the rights of the pastor of the mother church.[20]

Sometimes the priest permanently in charge of the vicarage is also vested with the entire radical responsibility as well as with its exercise.[21] In this latter case, as is pointed out by a writer in the *Periodica,* in all respects except in name the vicar is to be considered a true pastor.[22] Maroto, in describing vicarages of this kind as they exist in Canada, observes that the foundation of the distinction between them and true parishes lies in accidental extrinsic causes and circumstances, and not in any intrinsic differentiation. The matter can be compared to the distinction between a diocese and a prelacy *nullius,* or to that between a vicariate and a prefecture apostolic.[23]

Some authors include another type of permanent vicarage, namely that which belongs to the priest actually exercising parochial jurisdiction in a territory whose real pastor is a college, for example the cathedral chapter or a monastery. Canon 1427, however, distinguishes permanent vicarages from true parishes by naming the two disjunctively. Clearly, on account of its union with a collegiate moral person such a parish *contains* a vicarage, but it does not thereby itself *become* one: it remains a parish even though it must be administered by a vicar whether he be permanent or temporary. The union of a parish or vicarage with a collegiate moral person, although it results in the appointment of a vicar, does not seem to be what is contemplated in canon 1427.

A mere chapel of ease may not be called a vicarage even though it be attended by a curate *(vicarius cooperator)* who has been appointed to care for the people in the section of the parish sur-

[20] Pirhing, *Ius Canonicum,* lib. I, tit., 28. nn. 3-19, esp. n. 5; Schmalzgrueber, *Jus Ecclesiasticum,* lib. I, tit. 28, nn. 2-6.

[21] Reiffenstuel, *Jus Canonicum Universum,* lib. I, t. 28, nn. 29 ff., esp. n. 44.

[22] "De canone 1427 et de vicariis perpetuis."—*Periodica,* XIV (1925), p. (12)-(17).

[23] *Apollinaris,* VI (1933), 423-431, n. 15, 16.

rounding the chapel.[24] The reason is because it is not juridically distinct from the parish of which it forms a part. Furthermore, canon 476, § 8, prescribes that when satisfactory service cannot be rendered by the appointment of assistants, the bishop should provide according to canon 1427, i. e., by founding either new parishes or vicarages.

The process for establishing new vicarages is the same as that for establishing parishes.

NON-TERRITORIAL FORMS

Where the essentials of the faith are concerned, the Holy See is, of course, unyielding in demanding absolutely uniform creed and practice; but where it is a question of discipline she follows the policy that best promotes the welfare of souls. The Church has always been aware that ecclesiastical customs are not necessarily universal or immutable, so long as there is unity of Christian doctrine and teaching. That is the reason why provision is made in her law for exceptional forms of parochial organization in cases where the normal territorial plan is not sufficient for the satisfactory care of certain souls.

Because the Church is eager to preserve intact all the beautiful and ancient liturgies of the Orient as well as the Latin liturgy wherever there are sufficient numbers of Oriental Catholics living in Latin territory, she makes provision that these latter may worship according to their time-honored customs. On account of practical difficulties, and because the Chuch prefers not to obligate the Orientals to follow Occidental custom and law, even when they live in the Occident, she does not prescribe a strictly territorial organization for them, but by special indults she provides them with personal parishes. Such Oriental parishes do not come directly within the sphere of the Code.[25] All the parishes based on diversity of rite are not, however, Oriental. In the city of Toledo, Spain, for instance, there are non-territorial parishes in

[24] In accordance with canon 476, § 2.

[25] Duskie, John A., *The Canonical Status of the Orientals in the United States*, p. 55.

which members are enrolled upon the principle of rite—the very ancient Mozarabic rite which had been preserved by the Christians who remained in the city after its capture by the Arabs, and which has been maintained by their descendants ever since.[26]

Due to the inability of many immigrants who belong to the Latin rite to speak the language of the place in which they reside, some special provision must be made for pastoral care among them, if their spiritual needs are to be adequately administered. This can best be accomplished if they are grouped together under a pastor of their own nationality, who exercises over them the same jurisdiction as other pastors exercise over their flocks. Both the fact that the Holy See reserves to itself the right to erect or to suppress parishes using a language not generally spoken in the locality, and the implication of canon 216 that there should normally be one pastor in each territory exercising exclusive jurisdiction therein, indicate that such parishes are considered to be somewhat abnormal in the organization of the Church.[27] Parishes based on diversity of language are essentially personal, but they may also have territorial limits as a secondary principle of division, even though as a result two pastors hold territorial jurisdiction in the same place. The Holy See sees no incongruity in pastors having cumulative jurisdiction in the same territory.[28] Language parishes are most numerous in the United States, where they are quite commonly called national parishes.

There is less reason for the existence of purely national parishes based not on the difference of language but on the diversity of nations from which colonies have taken their origin, especially if the parishioners speak the same language as their neighbors. Such

[26] Ferreres, *Institutiones Canonicae*, I, n. 732.

[27] For special discussion see chapter VI, article 2, of this work.

[28] S. C. C., Feb. 1, 1908: "Ubinam et quomodo parochi qui, territorium exclusive proprium non habentes, cumulative territorium cum alio vel aliis parochis retinent, matrimoniis assistere valeant. Resp: Affirmative in territorio cumulative habito."—ASS, XLI (1908), 109, 111. For discussion of the territorial nature of language parishes see *Amer. Eccles. Review,* LXXX (1929), 88-94.

parishes do, however, exist, notably in Rome.[29] Of this same character are the racial parishes established to care for Negroes and Indians in the United States.[30]

Parishes exclusively for certain families or persons are rare. As the name indicates, the source from which they arise is some personal quality or achievement of particular groups, such as noble birth, for which the privilege of exemption from the territorial parish of their place of residence has been granted. In some instances eligible persons participate in membership in their own personal or family parish no matter where they reside; in other instances only when they are within a certain territory.[31]

Whether military chaplains are to be regarded as personal pastors depends upon the special arrangements made by the Holy See in different countries. The Code contains no formal provision regarding their status.[32]

[29] Maroto, *Institutiones Iuris Canonici,* II, n. 776.

[30] See chapter VI, article 2, of this work.

[31] Maroto, *l. c.*

[32] Can. 451, § 3. Cf. Ayrinhac, *Constitution of the Church in the New Code of Canon Law,* p. 304.

CHAPTER II

HISTORICAL SYNOPSIS

Section I. Apostolic and Post-Apostolic Period

In the first days of the Church, even though the Apostles made conversions very rapidly, they must nevertheless have been handicapped by the scarcity of co-laborers with the proper qualifications and competence to minister to the faithful scattered throughout the world. Consequently, they instructed and trained the most promising neophytes with special care, and imposing hands on them, transmitted to them the episcopal character and entrusted to them the responsibility of shepherding the new Church.[1]

St. Paul thus left Titus in Crete, with instructions to ordain other priests in the other cities of that district.[2] Abundant testimony of this practice can be found in the Acts of the Apostles,[3] and in the Epistles of St. Paul.[4] This frequent mention of bishops and churches in the more important cities nowhere includes a reference to churches outside of the cities in the smaller towns or villages of suburban districts. The type of organization in the cities can at best be surmised from the words of the Sacred Scriptures, for no information is given as to the number of clergy therein, or as to their functions. It is safe to say with Ferraris that there were no distinct parishes, but that the bishop took care of the souls of his church by means of priests whom he assigned or removed at will. He assigned to each of these priests whatever means of livelihood he thought sufficient.[5]

[1] Thomassinus, *Vetus et Nova Ecclesiae Disciplina,* pars I, lib. II, cap. XXI, n. 1.

[2] *Titus,* I, 5.

[3] *Acts,* XIV, 22; XX, 28-30.

[4] *Colos.,* IV, 17; I *Tim.,* VI, 22.

[5] Ferraris, F. Lucius, *Bibliotheca Canonica Juridica Moralis Theologica nec non Ascetica Polemica Rubricistica Historica,* "parochia," n. 7.

The sources yield no satisfactory evidence that even the embyronic outline of parish organization existed for nearly two centuries after the time of the Apostles. It seems instead that the practice of the Apostles[6] continued to prevail until it was no longer practicable in a much more populous church..[7] Having reached such a conclusion chiefly negatively, from lack of evidence to the contrary, historians propose it and develop it with some hesitation. As a matter of fact priests and deacons are mentioned so often that their useful existence was obviously normal in the life of the Church. But they were only minor ministers who had no directly official responsibility for the care of souls. The bishop probably continued to be the sole pastor in his diocese. Probably he alone was vested with authority therein, being assisted by the priests and deacons. The 38th canon of the *Canones Apostolorum* possibly could be taken literally when it says: "Let priests and deacons do nothing without the direction *(sententia)* of their bishop; it is he to whom the people of God have been entrusted, and from whom the account of their souls is required.[8] There is nothing in the sources to disprove the theory that this canon describes the universal practice, whereas there is much repetition to support the view that the canon cited describes the situation quite accurately. For instance, the recurrence of the same idea in the letters of St. Ignatius, Martyr (d. ca. 107), is so frequent as to rule out the likelihood of hyperbole. In fact he anticipates, chronologically, those very words when, at the beginning of the second century, he admonishes priests and laity alike to "do nothing without their bishop".[9]

[6] *Titus,* I, 5.

[7] Thomassinus, *Vetus et Nova Eccl. Disc.,* pars I, lib. II, cap. XXI, n. 1.

[8] MPG, CXXXVII, 119; Harduin, I, 19; Bruns, *Canones Apostolorum et Conciliorum,* I, 6.

[9] Cf. *Ep. ad Ephes., cap.* 4: ". . . Unde decet vos in episcopi sententiam concurrere, quod et facitis. Nam memorabile vestrum presbyterium dignum Deo ita cooptatum est episcopo ut chordae citharae."—Kirch, *Enchiridion Fontium Historiae Ecclesiae Antiquae,* n. 19; Lightfoot, *Apostolic Fathers,* Part II, Vol. III, 23. *Ep. ad Phil.,* cap. 7: ". . . Spiritus autem praedicavit,

So closely is the community bound to its bishop, its only pastor, that its members must attend his cathedral for divine services, and must receive the sacraments from him.[10]

It is not until after he begins dealing with the IV century that the historian finds any solid affirmative evidence on which to base his conclusions, and even then he finds that the paucity of documents for the succeeding early centuries continues to be a source of only incomplete satisfaction.

Section II. Gradual Historical Development of Territorial Districts Independent of each other but Dependent on the Bishop

Art. 1. *The Problem of the Bishops at Beginning of IV Century.*

With the extensive spread of the faith new bishoprics became necessary and were supplied without the need of changing the old discipline, but when that spread became intensive, resulting in a relatively dense Christian population, the

dicens haec: Sine Episcopo nihil faciatis . . ."—Lightfoot, *op. cit.*, Part II, Vol. III, 36; MPG, V, 701.

[10] Ep. St. Ignatii, *Ad Magnes.*, cap. 7, 2: "Omnes adunati ad templum Dei concurrite, sicut ad unum altare."—MPG, V, 668; *Ad Smyr.*, cap. 8, 1: ". . . separatim ab episcopo nemo quidquam faciat eorum quae ad ecclesiam spectant. Valida eucharistia habeatur illa, quae sub episcopo peragitur, vel sub eo cui ipse concesserit."—Rouet de Journel, *Enchiridion Patristicum*, n. 65; MPG, V, 713; *Ibid.*, cap. 8, 2: ". . . non licet sine episcopo neque baptizare neque agapen celebrare; sed quodcumque ille probaverit, hoc et Deo est beneplacitum, ut firmum et validum sit omne quod peragitur."—Journel, *loc. cit.*, MPG, *loc. cit. Ad Philadelph.*, cap. 4: "Studeatis igitur una eucharistia uti: una enim est caro Domini nostri Jesu Christi et unus calix in unitatem sanguinis ipsius, unum altare, sicut unus episcopus cum presbyterio et diaconis, conservis meis; ut, quod faciatis, secundum Deum faciatis,"—Journel, *op. cit.*, n. 56. St. Justin, Martyr, *Apologia I*, 65: "Qui fratribus praeest . . . preces et eucharistiam absolvit . . . et qui apud nos dicuntur diaconi panem et vinum et aquam . . . unicuique praesentium participanda distribuunt, et ad absentes perferunt."—Kirch, *Enchiridion Fontium*, n. 54. *Apologia II*, n. 67: "Ac Solis, ut dicitur, de omnum sive urbes sive agros incolentium in eundem locum fit conventus et commentaria apostolorum, aut scripta prophetarum leguntur, quoad licet per tempus."—Kirch, *op. cit.*, *n.* 56.

old order was inadequate to meet the new conditions. A bishop could care personally for a small community; but the time arrived when the community became too numerous to be accommodated at the cathedral church, namely, when conversions were made beyond the suburbs of the cities and in the more distant small villages.[1] When the task of caring personally for so large and so scattered a flock began to exceed the ability of the most capable bishops, the bishops began to share their responsibilites with their clergy by sending them out to form new, subordinate centers of worship.

This need did not spring up simultaneously in all places, because the growth of the Church which was responsible for it was not equally rapid in all places. Near the cities which were most populous and which covered the greatest area, and in which the seeds of the faith had first been sown, it as a rule developed soonest; whereas near smaller cities it was not acute until many years later. It was undoubtedly delayed in the West, especially in the vicinity of Rome, by the savage persecutions before the Edict of Constantine (313).

The widespread need for a change in the old order could not have been detected at once by Christendom as a whole. It rather became the new and personal problem of each bishop individually, or of neighboring bishops collectively, who had to work out a solution according to their own judgment. Individually, or in local councils, without the help of universal Church law, they evolved plans that seemed best adapted to their own locality. Uniform universal law did not therefore make the practice: the practice eventually led to general law centuries later.

The actual evolution of the parish system must be searched

[1] Tertullian, *Apologeticum,* I: "Obsessam vociferantur civitatem in agris, in castellis, in insulis Christianis."—MPL, I, 262; *Adv. Jud.*, cap. 7—MPL, I. 611; Lactantius, *de mort. persec.*, n. 3: "nullus esset terrarum angulus tam remotus quo non religio Dei penetrasset."—*Corpus Vindobonense,* XXVII, 2, 2, p. 177; MPL, VII, 200. Pliny the Younger, *Epist. X,* 97: "neque enim civitates tantum, sed vicos etiam atque agros superstitionis istius contagio pervagata est."

out in the separate locations in which it began. Particular legislation must be examined to see what can be discovered and inferred about the manner as well as the rapidity of the free and uneven growth. It is often hard to evaluate the records left behind, because many of them do not directly represent parish legislation at all but merely offer the *obiter dicta* of contemporary writers. The very terminology is utterly confusing. Consequently, much unavoidable obscurity veils the history.

Art. 2. *Early Development of Parochial System in the Orient.*

To the Orient belongs the distinction of having produced the first unmistakable signs of parish organization, along with certain earlier evidences of a more or less doubtful character in this regard. A certain document would give Rome clear parochial legislation even before the East had any, but this document has been rejected for reasons to be seen later.[2]

The first doubtful indication of parochial organization in the East is to be found in a passage of the Ecclesiastical History of Eusebius of Caesarea, who relates that Dionysius, bishop of Alexandria, when he was exiled into the interior of Egypt, found near a hamlet called Arsinoë, priests with whom he held a conference for three days, and who performed religious services.[3] Not enough is known about these Egyptian priests to say that they were parish priests. They could have been missionaries with a certain stability in that place, working as the emissaries of some more or less distant bishop, or they may have been the assistants of a rural bishop living in their midst.[4]

There is good reason to believe that the initial break in the pristine unity of administration within the bishopric began with the advent of clerics known as land-bishops who as Zorell thinks, were identical with the *chorepiscopi* who became so

[2] See footnote 29, *infra.*

[3] *Hist. Eccl.*, Lib. VII, cap. 11 and cap. 24—MPG, XX, 671 and 695.

[4] Bastnagel, *Appointment of Parochial Adjutants and Assistants,* p. 6.

prominent in the East in the IV century.[5] The oldest document that makes mention of "land-bishops" is the encyclical letter which the bishops of the Council of Antioch directed against Paul of Samosata about the year 270.[6] The *chorepiscopi* were expressly mentioned by name for the first time at the Synod of Ancyra (314), can. 13.[7] The very manner of dealing with the *chorepiscopi* in this council proves that they were already a strongly entrenched institution in the Church because the council finds it necessary to curb their practice of assuming powers that belong rightfully only to the city bishops. Surely the usurpation proscribed in the canon, namely, the ordaining of priests and deacons, required considerable time to develop before it became an abuse. How long a time that was there is no way of knowing. The ecumenical Council of Nicea, in 325, presupposes the widespread existence of these land-bishops when it provides in canon 8 that the Novatian bishops who had returned to the profession of orthodoxy should be instituted as *chorepiscopi.*[8]

It cannot be said definitely that these *chorepiscopi* were real pastors in a modern sense. The precise nature of their status and position has remained a matter of dispute among authorities. Whether they were actual bishops with limited jurisdiction, or whether they were priests with more powers than the usual ones, theirs was not a separate order distinct from others. Rather it was an ecclesiastical office committed, at least sometimes, to bishops.[9] They apparently held an intermediate position: having less authority than the bishop, for they were sub-

[5] "Die Entwickelung des Parochialsystems bis zum Ende der Karolingerzeit," *AkKR,* LXXXII (1902), 74-98, and 258-89, esp. page 80 for testimony cited.

[6] Eusebius, *Hist. Eccl.,* VII, 30—MPG, XX, 709; *Kirch, Enchiridion* (1914), n. 325. The words used are "ἐπισκόπους τῶν ὁμόρων ἀγρῶν τέ καὶ πόλεων."

[7] Harduin, I, 277; cf. also can. 13 of Council of Neocaesarea—Harduin, I, 286.

[8] Mansi, II, 671-72; Harduin, I, 326.

[9] Bingham, *Antiquities of the Christian Church,* Vol. I, bk. II, cap. 14, par. 4.

ject to a city bishop, and more than the priest, for they had the position of vicars of the bishop in certain individual functions, and they had the duty of overseeing the country clerics.[10]

The priests living with the *chorepiscopi* in a sort of community life were utterly dependent upon his will for the exercise of their spiritual functions. In the presence of him or of city priests they could not celebrate Mass on Sunday or distribute Communion: they could do so only when he was unable to be present himself to celebrate, or where the town was too small to justify appointment of a bishop.[11] Further light is thrown on the functions of the *chorepiscopi* during the decades that followed. From canons 7 and 8 of the Synod of Gangra (ca. 330), it is clear that only the *chorepiscopus* himself or one of his appointees had the right to accept church dues, or to administer or distribute public offerings.[12] Clearly without these rights any of the subordinate clergy could scarcely have been true pastors! In 341 *chorepiscopi* were still forbidden to ordain men to Sacred Orders without first obtaining faculties from the bishop to whom they and their "posses-

[10] Council of Antioch (341), can. 10: "Qui in vicis vel possessionibus chorepiscopi nominantur, quamvis manus impositionem episcoporum perceperint (et ut episcopi consecrati sint), tamen sanctae synodo placuit, ut modum proprium recognoscant, ut gubernent sibi subjectas ecclesias, earumque moderamine curaque contenti sint. Ordinent etiam lectores, et subdiaconos, atque exorcistas: quibus promotiones istae sufficiant. Nec presbyterum vero, nec diaconum audeant ordinare, praeter civitatis episcopum, cui ipse cum possessione subjectus est . . . Chorepiscopum vero civitatis episcopus ordinet, cui ille subjectus est."—Kirch, *Enchiridion*, n. 494; Harduin, I, 597; Mansi, II, 1311.

[11] Council of Neocaesarea (314-325), can. 13: "Vicani autem presbyteri non possunt *in dominico* offerre praesente episcopo, vel urbis presbyteris; neque panem dare precationis, neque calicem. Si autem absint, et solus ad precationem vocatus fuerit, dat."—Mansi, II, 541-42. Harduin, (I, 286) gives variant translations of this canon. Cf. also Synod of Gangra (between 325-380), cc. 6-8—Harduin, I, 535; Synod of Antioch (341), can. 10—Harduin, I, 597; Synod of Sardica (343-44), can. 6—Mansi, III, 10; Harduin, I, 639.

[12] Harduin, I, 535.

sion" were subject.[13] On the other hand, they exercised personal direction over the exercise of spiritual functions by the clergy within their jurisdiction. Yet, whatever the juridical position and subsequent development of the institute of *chorepiscopi*, the fact is clear that even in the third century there were already special churches in the rural districts and special meetings or congregations of the faithful were held there.[14]

Two years after the Council of Antioch there is to be found in the Council of Sardica (343) an indication of some dissatisfaction with the practice of consecrating so many *chorepiscopi* for small hamlets, when simple priests could serve satisfactorily instead.[15] The result was that within a few decades, in the small scattered villages of the East which were neither in the neighborhood of a great city nor themselves sufficiently large to furnish the elements of a complete organization, presbyters were ordained and appointed to reside at them, but the bishops to oversee them were itinerant. These traveling bishops, *periodeutae*, are mentioned for the first time in the Council of Laodicea (between 343-381), which forbids the appointment of any other class of bishops in villages and country districts.[16]

The best authenticated example of early parochial development anywhere is found in the city of Alexandria and nearby. In the year 348 or 350, when St. Athanasius wrote his *Apologia contra Arianos*, there were in the neighborhood of Alexandria, in the district of Mareötes, Christians who were no longer expected to attend the bishop's cathedral church, but who met in separate buildings nearer their own residences. They were under the care of clerics who described themselves as "priests and deacons of Mareötes", and who write "in the name of the whole Church which is subject to the most reverend bishop

[13] Council of Antioch (341), can. 10. See footnote 10, above.

[14] Zorell, "Die Entwickelung des Parochialsystems bis zum Ende der Karolingerzeit," *AkKR*, LXXXII (1902), 74-78.

[15] Can. 6—Mansi, III, 10; Harduin, I, 639.

[16] Cf. can. 57—Harduin, I, 792.

Athanasius."[17] In this region of Mareötes there had never been a bishop or *chorepiscopus,* but the entire district was subject to the bishop of Alexandria. Each of ten or more priests had his own village to care for.[18]

St. Epiphanius, bishop of Constantia (Salamis) on the Island of Cyprus, reports at the end of the IV century that there were more churches in the neighborhood of Alexandria than there had been at the time of Arius,—and there had been many then.[19] Indeed, not only outside the city was this arrangement to be found, but within the very city itself each church had its own resident priest who took care of ecclesiastical affairs.[20] Analysis of these texts yields two different possibilities as to the nature of this non-episcopal care. The possibility that it might have been chorepiscopal is eliminated by St. Athanasius in one of the texts just cited. Hatch thinks that the Christians who lived outside the city and worshipped away from the cathedral are to be regarded as members of the bishop's own church, his parishioners. He maintains that these extra-urban churches were analogous to present day "chapels of ease".[21]

Quite as probable is the opinion that such churches themselves, not the cathedral church, were the parish churches of

[17] St. Athanasius, *Apologia contra Arianos,* I, 74—MPG, XXV, 386.

[18] St. Athanasius, *Apol. cont. Arianos,* I, 85—MPG, XXV, 399; See also I, 63: "Cum igitur Ecclesiae definitis in locis essent presbyteris omnibus conventus in iisdem Ecclesiis agentibus . . ."—MPG, XXV, 363.

[19] St. Epiphanius, *Adv. Haeres.,* LXVIII, 4: ". . . Arius enim Baucalae cuiusdam apud Alexandriam Ecclesiae presbyter erat. Nam unicuique ecclesiae, quae tum multae erant, hodie vero plures sunt, suus attribuebatur presbyter . . ."—MPG, XLII, 190.

[20] St. Epiphanius, *Adv. Haer.,* LXIX, 1: "Quotquot Alexandriae Catholicae communionis ecclesiae sunt uni archiepiscopo subiectae, suus cuique praepositus est presbyter, qui ecclesiastica munera iis administret, qui circa ecclesias illas habitant, eorumque conventicula vici, sive laurae, ab Alexandrinis vulgo nominantur."—MPG, XLII, 202.

[21] *The Organization of the Early Christian Churches,* (London: Longmans Green and Co., 1918), p. 198.

those living in their vicinity. In the absence of definite proof neither alternative compels acceptance.

Elsewhere than at Alexandria the customary rural practice was that which was maintained at Constantinople as described by Justinian, who mentions several churches in that metropolis which did not have their own clergy attached to them, but were served in courses by the priests of the cathedral church.[22]

By the time of the third ecumenical council, at Ephesus in 431, rural parochial churches had plainly become a permanent institution, since even an auxiliary priest was already needed in a certain village church.[23]

Twenty years later the council of Chalcedon (451) in canon 6 forbade the ordination of priests unless they were destined for a definite church. From canon 19 of the same council it is clear that two types of rural churches existed, one of which was parochial, and the other auxiliary.[24] Eastern parish discipline was crystallized by the time of the seventh ecumenical council at Nicea (787) in which it was decreed that clerics must not abandon the parishes for which they were ordained, in order to betake themselves to another without the consent of their bishops, nor is any cleric to preside at more than one church.[25]

Art. 3. *Exceptional Development of Parishes at Rome.*

It is not possible to describe the development of the parish system in the West precisely without examining each region separately. The reason is because every region worked out a system best adapted to its own needs. In the absence of any general law, one important factor in preserving a certain notable uniformity in such independent development was the esteem enjoyed by particular legislation even outside of the

[22] *Novels,* III, 1.

[23] Cf. Mansi, IV, 1357-58, where a certain Patricius, in the list of those who subscribed the acts of the council, is called the "second priest" of the village of Paradioxylon.

[24] Harduin, II, 603, 607.

[25] Can. 10 and 15—Mansi, XIII, 751, 753; Harduin, IV, 494, 495.

territory for which it was intended. Of themselves, the canons of particular councils had no universal binding force; nevertheless they were not only frequently copied, but often also they were followed in the more or less remote districts as soon as they became known.[26] The parallel systems which evolved were therefore similar in many respects, but they were not exact duplicates; in some instances they displayed marked dissimilarity.

Like Alexandria in the East, so Rome in the West was the only episcopal city which probably possessed parish organization before the year 1000, and it is not without some hesitation that authors interpret the Roman system as truly parochial.[27] In the Eternal City churches were apportioned under the name of "*titles*" to priests who became known as "*cardinales.*"

According to the *Liber Pontificalis* there was in ancient Rome a quasi-parochial system beginning as early as the first decade of the II century, when Pope St. Evaristus (99-107) divided the *titles* in the city of Rome among priests.[28]

This same *Liber Pontificalis* contains a letter ascribed to Pope Dionysius (259-268), in which he is said to have divided the churches and cemeteries among priests, and to have attached to these churches the care of souls and to have set definite parish boundaries. This text has been reproduced in the *Decretum Gratiani.*[29] Unfortunately, while the meaning of the text is quite clear, the authority on which the document rests is not worthy of confidence. Dionysius' apparent duplication of the work already accomplished by Evaristus may perhaps

[26] Cicognani, *Canon Law,* (Philadelphia: Dolphin Press, 1935), p. 173.

[27] Hinschius, *System des katholischen Kirchenrechts,* II, 277-278. Although Hinschius recognizes the multiplicity of places of worship in Rome and Alexandria, he is unwilling to concede that there was any parochial division of the territory of the bishops in either of these two cities.

[28] In Vita Evaristi Papae—Mansi, I, 621.

[29] *Liber Pontificalis,* Ep. I Dionysii ad Sever.—Mansi, I, 1006; c. 1, C. XIII, q. 2.

be explained by the disruption of ecclesiastical order and discipline resulting from the persecutions under Decius and Valerian. Of better authority, but insufficiently precise in details, is the historian Eusebius, who reproduces a letter of Pope Cornelius (251-253) to Fabius, bishop of Antioch, stating that there were at that time forty-six presbyters in Rome.[30]

In other words, an ecclesiastical division of the city for various parochial purposes is attributed to popes of the second and third centuries. The persecutions and the resulting disruption of the work of the predecessors of Pope Marcellus I (308-309) may reasonably be assumed in explanation of his fresh division of the city into 25 *titles* as parishes, constituted for the sake of administering baptism and penance to the multitudes converted from paganism,[31] and for the burial of the marytrs. Long after this the number of *titles* stood at twenty-eight, when obviously the increased enrolment of members implies a greater number of places of worship. The priests attached to these *tituli* came to be known as *cardinales,* a name previously used elsewhere in the provinces, whereas the Roman clergy attached to other churches obtained no such name.[32]

St. Optatus in 370, half a century after the Edict of Constantine, mentions that there were more than forty basilicas in the city of Rome, from which it is easy to infer that there was one priest for each of them, and probably more for the papal basilica.[33]

Such an ecclesiastical division, however obscure its beginning, was an accomplished fact at the end of the V century.

[30] Eusebius, *Historia Ecclesiastica,* VI, 43—MPG, XX, 615.,

[31] *Liber Pontificalis,* In Vita Marcelli, P.—Mansi, I, 1259.

[32] From these ancient documents few conclusions of unimpeachable certainty can be drawn. They may indeed be genuine sources, but modern research has undermined their foundations. The section of the *Liber Pontificalis* dealing with the lives of the Popes prior to Anastasius II (496-498) is generally unreliable, and therefore of little value in determining historical details. See Kirsch, "Liber Pontificalis", *Catholic Encyclopedia,* IX, 224.

[33] *De Schism. Donat.* II, 4—*Corpus Vindobonense,* XXVI, 39; MPL, XI, 954.

To vouch for it there are the signatures of the Roman presbyters at the Council of Rome, in 499, under Pope Symmachus.[34]

There had been the practice of only one consecration of the Eucharist in the infant community of Rome. The Pope seems to have said the only Mass in the city, but employed the local acolytes for the honored task of carrying the Sacred Species to the other churches of the city, a practice calculated to impress on the minds of the faithful the unity of the Christian body. However, in cemeteries and churches distant from the basilica of the Pope, the priests were allowed to consecrate.[35] The existence of such a practice is enough to prevent authorities from unanimously holding the opinion that the Roman organization was truly parochial. It does seem strange that places of worship which otherwise seem to have all the characteristics of parish churches should not have Mass on Sundays.

Art. 4. *Rural Parochial Development in the Occident.*

Of the external circumstances that contributed to the formation of the modern parish probably one of the most influential was the pattern of the Western Empire in the midst of which this canonical institution developed. Especially is this so in Spain and Gaul where the earliest Christians were almost entirely resident among the inhabitants of Roman towns. Hatch thinks that these towns, which were seldom situated off the lines of the great military roads, were the civilized centers

[34] Mansi, VIII, 236.

[35] Innocent I, *Epist. ad Decentium*, cap. 5: "De fermento vero quod die Dominica per titulos mittimus, superflue nos consulere voluisti, cum omnes ecclesiae nostrae intra civitatem sint constitutae. Quarum presbyteri quia die ipsa propter plebem sibi creditam nobiscum convenire non possunt, idcirco Fermentum a nobis confectum per Acolythos accipiunt, ut se a nostra communione maxime illa die non iudicent separatos. Quod per parochias fieri debere non puto, quia nec longe portanda sunt Sacramenta, nec nos per Coemeteria diversa constitutis Presbyteris destinamus et presbyteri eorum conficiendorum ius habeant atque licentiam."—Mansi, III, 1030.

of semi-civilized districts, and that they became episcopal sees and the headquarters for missionary activity.[36]

If his opinions conform to fact, one would expect to find well defined instances of parallelism in the evolution of ecclesiastical institutions within the boundaries of an empire with political unity and relatively easy intercommunication. One would expect the Church to have similar problems where the local civil government followed a pattern laid down for an expire, where the people's problems were much the same, and where it was relatively easy to exchange ideas.

It is not surprising, therefore, that the first definite signs of parish economy in Spain and in Gaul appear within a decade of one another, at the beginning of the IV century. At the Council of Elvira (held between the years 300 and 306) the acts were subscribed by a group of priests in a manner which shows that they belonged to places outside the episcopal city.[37]

With this very council begins a series of legislation on residence that is both obvious and significant among the sketchy and obscure duties that are assigned to parish priests before the time of Charlemagne. Canon 18 requires these priests to remain permanently attached to their districts and to reside in them.[38] Apparently abuses and evasions of the law had begun to creep in by the time of the first Council of Tarragona (516), for the Spanish bishops were then compelled to reassert with the threat of canonical penalties the obligation incumbent on parish clergy to reside at their parish churches, lest by their absence they deprive the people of religious ministrations. It seems that priest and deacon were allowed to alternate in their

[36] *The Organization of the Early Christian Churches,* p. 201. He lists the great Roman metropolises and municipalities that became bishoprics and retained that dignity until the present time, including Sens, Paris, Rouen, Charters.

[37] "Restitutus, presbyter de Elpel; Natalis, presbyter de Orsuna; Maurus, presbyter de Illiturgi; . . . etc."—Mansi, II, 29. Thomassinus, *Vetus et Nova Ecclesiae Disciplina,* pars I, lib. II, cap. 22, n. 8, suspects the authenticity of these signatures.

[38] Mansi, II, 9.

week-day services at these country churches. For the weekly solemn service priest and deacon alike with the lesser clerics were expected to be on hand.[39] The effect of the canonical penalties may have been to make the priests themselves less inclined to desert their own churches, but the law seems to have been frustrated by the bishops themselves, if one is to judge by the restriction placed on the bishops by the council of Seville (619). The fathers present were imbued with the conviction that a priest was ordained for a specific congregation, and that he should remain to minister to that group, unless it was for the best interests of the Church that he be sent elsewhere. To this end they decreed that the bishop was not to transfer priests arbitrarily, nor without first consulting his council.[40]

But forces beyond the control of either a devoted bishop or a zealous priest could still deprive the community of the attention it needed. The volume of work might be too burdensome; sickness, or incapacity from other causes could hinder the work of the pastor. Some French bishops in such circumstances had apparently simply appointed additional priests to the church with administrative powers equal to those held by the priest already in possession. Their practice was condemned.[41] No other solution was offered until in 675 the

[39] Can. 7: "De diocesanis ecclesiis, vel clero id placuit definiri, ut presbyteri, vel diaconi, qui inibi constituti sunt, cum clericis, septimanas observent: id est ut presbyter unam faciat hebdomadam; qua expleta succedat ei diaconus similiter: ea scilicet conditione servata, ut omnis clerus die sabbato ad vesperam sit paratus, quo facilius die dominico solemnitas cum omnium praesentia celebretur: ita tamen ut omnibus diebus vesperas et matutinas celebrent: quia desistente clero (quod est pessimum) comperimus in basilicis nec luminaria ministrari . . . "—Mansi, VIII; 542.

[40] Can. 6—Mansi, X. 558-59.

[41] Council of Reims, can. 19: "Sicut in unaquaque ecclesia unus presbyter debet esse, ita ipsa, quae sponsa vel uxor eius dicitur non potest dividi inter plures presbyteros, sed unum tantummodo habebit sacerdotem, qui eam caste et sincere regat. Unde interdicimus ut nullus praesumat ecclesiam inter duos, vel plures dividere, quia ecclesia Christi uxor et sponsa esse debet, non scortum, sicut Calixtus papa testatur."—Mansi,

eleventh council of Toledo ordered priests to obtain helpers wherever a sufficient number of auxiliary priests was available.[42] It is not the purpose of this work to discover the manner in which these assistant priests obtained a status which had been looked on with disfavor by the Church, as is evidenced by the Council of Chalcedon[43] and later was reaffirmed in almost identical words by the capitulary of Aix-la-Chapelle (789).[44] These rulings are more in accord with the other foregoing legislation of the Church to the effect that every priest should be attached to a definite church.

The actual duties of the resident parochial clergy are only partly known. They could, for instance, baptize within their parish, and they could superintend any baptism administered therein by a deacon. They were granted the faculty of reconciling the sick and the dying, but not ordinary penitents.[45] The Chrism was not to be blessed by them, but rather it must be obtained annually before Easter by the pastor of every church in the diocese. This applied to country priests as well as to others.[46]

At this same time in Italy and far-off Africa similar legislation was being enacted. Pope Innocent I in the Roman synod of

X, 603. Mansi quotes the canon from c. 4, C. XXI, q. 2 of the Decree of Gratian. The date of the council seems to fall between 624 and 630. Some think it to be identical with a council held at Clichy in 626 or 627. (Cf. Ott, "Reims, Synods of," *Cath. Encycl.*, XII, 730).

[42] Can. 14—Mansi, XI, 145; Harduin, III, 1029.

[43] Can. 6—Harduin, II, 603.

[44] Can. 25: "Nullum absolute ordinari, neque presbyterum, nec diaconum, neque penitus quemquam eorum qui sunt in Ecclesiae ordine nisi specialiter ecclesiae civitatis, vel vici, vel martyrii, qui ordinandus est fuerit declaratus. Horum autem ordinationem huiusmodi, qui absolute ordinantur constituit sancta synodus *inefficacem* esse, et numquam posse ad ordinantis iniuriam praevalere."—Harduin, IV, 833. Cf. also cc. 1-2, D. 70.

[45] Council of Elvira (300-306), cans. 77 and 32—Mansi, II, 18 and 11; Harduin, I, 258 and 253.

[46] I Council of Toledo (400), can. 20—Mansi, III, 1002; Harduin, I, 992. See I Council of Vaison (442), can. 3,—Mansi, VI, 453.

the year 402 granted to priests the right to baptize,[47] and in his letter to Bishop Decentius he grants to rural priests the right to offer the Holy Sacrifice for those who dwell beyond reasonable traveling distance of the cathedral.[48] The second council of Carthage (390), on the contrary, withheld from priests the faculty of blessing oils, of consecrating virgins and of reconciling public sinners at services over which the bishop presided. Privately, however, the priest could reconcile sinners.[49] In the third council of Carthage (397) the prohibition against consecrating virgins was removed.[50] The duty of preaching was imposed on priests by the second council of Vaison (529), which adds that if they are prevented by sickness from fulfiling this obligation a deacon is to supply their place by reading one of the homilies of the Fathers.[51]

A brief review of the foregoing legislation of the Western Church shows that the parochial organization of the East and West had reached the same stage of development by the end of the eighth century. Rome had its city parishes, probably. Alexandria also had them. The council of Nice in the year 787 had insisted that clerics were to be permanently attached to the churches for which they were ordained, and that they were not to exercise the pastoral office in more than one church.[52]

In the West it had been decreed about the year 630 that a parish was to have only one pastor;[53] and in the year 789 absolute ordination of clerics, that is, without their being attached to some benefice, was condemned.[54]

[47] Can. 7—Mansi, III, 1137. Cf. Thomassinus, *Vetus et Nova Ecclesiae Disciplina,* pars I, lib. II, cap. 23, n. 7.

[48] See footnote 35, *supra.*

[49] Can. 3 and 4—Mansi, III, 693.

[50] Can. 36—Mansi, III, 885.

[51] Can. 2—Mansi, VIII, 727.

[52] Can. 10, 15—Harduin, IV, 769-70.

[53] Council of Reims, can. 19—Mansi, X, 603.

[54] Capitulary of Aix-la-Chapelle, can. 25—Harduin, IV, 833.

Art. 5. *City Parishes Outside of Rome*

Authors agree that Rome and Alexandria were the only two probable exceptions to the general rule that until about the year 1000 there were no parishes in episcopal cities, but that the bishop continued to be the only pastor in the city. Wherever the word *"paroecia"* refers to parochial division in the legislation of those ages, it is always taken to mean rural parishes. From the abundance of texts that are available, a few suffice to show that "city" and "parish" were mutually exclusive and contrasted.[55]

An unusually strong negative argument to support the same conclusion is drawn from the fact that there are no monuments whatever of city parishes before the year 1000. Marius Lupi is convincing when he declares that the most exhaustive research has failed utterly to produce any evidence whatever that such parishes did exist. If the records of city parishes ever existed, the probability that they have been lost is almost negligible, because the extant documents of those times dealing with rural parishes are very numerous; and because, of the total number of monuments of other kinds from those times, many more belong to the cities than to the country; because there are abundant indications of parishes in the cities of Rome and Alexandria.[56]

In regard to those countries where the Germans founded their empire the lack of city parishes is all the more easily to be presumed, because the cities were smaller and less densely populated than the important centers of the ancient world. Indeed, the fact that the Frankish sources always put the rural parishes in opposition not to city parishes but to the city itself with its surrounding territory, and the fact that they

[55] Bouix, *De Parocho*, p. 28, ff. Council of Agde (506), can. 21—Mansi, VIII, 328; Harduin, II, 1000; Council of Auvergne (535), can. 15—Harduin, II, 1182; Council of Trosly (909), can 6—Mansi, XVIII A, 279; c. 33, c. XVI, 2. 1.

[56] Marius Lupi, *De Paroeciis ante annum Millesimum*, dissert. 2, cap. 10, cited by Bouix in his work, *De Parocho*, p. 33.

show the episcopal church itself to be the normal place for regular divine services, are of decisive moment against any theory of a division of cities into parishes.[57]

The earliest indication that city parishes were coming into being is found in the council of Limoges in 1031 or 1032. Indications are given in this council that there was a weakening of the old discipline under which the bishop had been the sole pastor of the city, and had accomplished his duties with the assistance of the community of clerics living with him. The text of the acts of the council shows that there were other baptismal churches within the city besides the cathedral church; and the context shows clearly that the new organization enjoyed the approval of the bishops present.[58] Elsewhere in the same text it is implied that preaching was undertaken in other churches besides the cathedral. The conditions of the times—the tendencies to schism during the eleventh and twelfth centuries, the fact that many bishops-elect remained without episcopal consecration for a long time, the fact that even archpriests in cathedrals were often not even in sacred orders, the scarcity of priests to attend to the needs of the faithful—were responsible for many bishops conniving at the assumption of parochial duties by the priests who were scattered through the minor churches in the city.[59]

However, until the council of Trent, the status of city parishes remained obscure. Their boundaries were vague; their functions were ill-defined; and their very existence was not universal.[60]

[57] Hinschius, *System des katholischen Kirchenrechts,* II, 278, 279.

[58] Session II: ". . . et hi qui in aliis ecclesiis apud hanc civitatem baptizantur, ipso die coram episcopo ad confirmationem in hac sede cum luminaribus exhibeantur."—Mansi, XIX, 543.

[59] Marius Lupi, *De Paroeciis ante Millesimum, dissert.* 2, cap. 10, cited in Bouix, *De Parocho,* p. 43.

[60] Hinschius, *System des katholischen Kirchenrechts,* II, 281.

Section III. Growth of Legislation

Art. 1. *Before the Council of Trent*

An institution that eventually played an important part in parish history was that of having oratories in private houses, of which some were open to the public, and in monasteries where Mass was said and where the sacraments were administered. This institution was important because it was widespread, but apparently it never was made the starting-point universally for the founding of parishes in the Catholic world.

Division of the land into villages was augmented by the political rise of the Germanic peoples, who tended to live in villages rather than in cities, thus necessitating the division of the diocese into smaller parts. Rich families who were too far removed from the cities began, more universally than in the earlier centuries, to build chapels in their houses, and since they owned the houses, they also assigned the priests who were to minister in them. The number of these chapels increased as the Frankish kings cultivated more and greater stretches of land.[1] The council of Orleans (541) implies that with the permission of the bishop Mass could be celebrated in private oratories of masters of estates.[2] From that time until the time of the council of Trent numerous laws were enacted by councils approving and regulating the practice of saying Mass in oratories.[3] Although the administration of the sacraments was usually forbidden in oratories,[4] thus unmistakably showing that most of them were not parish churches from the beginning, yet it seems that private chapels were not always reserved for the convenience of the owners of estates, because some of them seem to have had districts assigned to them, and

[1] Zorell, "Entwicklung des Parochialsystems," AkKR, LXXXII (1902), 259.

[2] Can. 7—Mansi, IX, 114.

[3] For a lengthy list of such laws see Feldhaus, *Oratories*, Washington: Catholic University of America, 1929, p. 34-35.

[4] Feldhaus, *op. cit.*, p. 38-45.

so seem to have become country parishes. Hence the fourth council of Orleans, in the year 541, speaks of "*paroeciae* in potentum domibus", and it says: "Si quis in agro suo aut habet aut postulet dioecesim . . . ,"[5] and the ninth council of Toledo, in the year 655 deals with the case of "ecclesiae paroeciales" which had been founded by private persons,[6] but of course, with the permission of the bishop.[7]

In the previously cited canon 33 of the council of Orleans is contained a highly significant element in regard to oratories. It is the requirement that they be sufficiently endowed with land and with appropriate means of livelihood for the clerics who are to conduct and perform the divine services.[8] The Emperor Justinian incorporated an identical statute into the civil law of the empire during the same decade (ca. 540). Furthermore, he insisted that the consent of the bishop be obtained beforehand. Going even farther he forbade the celebration of Mass in private houses, although he encouraged the designation of private oratories for private worship without the celebration therein of the Sacred Mysteries.[9]

Due to the fact that religious should not leave their monasteries even to take part in the solemn festivities at the parish church on the principal feasts of the year, they were granted the right of celebrating Mass in their own oratories even on days when the privilege was denied to other chapels. Many of the faithful conveniently availed themselves of the opportunity to fulfil their obligation in the monastery chapel, without ever attending their parish church. Hence, various councils of the middle ages sought to counteract this practice either by forbidding the faithful to attend Mass in the chapels of religious on Sundays and the principal feast days, or by ordering the religious to refuse admission to the laity, or finally,

[5] Can. 26 and 33—Mansi, IX, 117 and 119.

[6] Cap 2—Mansi, XI, 26.

[7] Council of Orleans (511), can. 17—Harduin, II, 1011; *Novellae*, 67, 2.

[8] See above, footnote 5.

[9] *Novellae*, LVIII, 58, pr.; LXVII, 1 and 2.

by ordering that Mass be celebrated at an hour too inconvenient for outsiders.[10]

The laws just cited do not mean, however, that the monks never took care of the souls near their monasteries, for they did.[11] Indeed, the monasteries often founded their own chapels and churches, and they often inherited newly founded churches from others as gifts, which in the course of time also acquired parochial rights. In addition to that the bishops themselves, as a consequence of the religious fervor of the times, gave over to the monasteries many existing parochial churches with their income as their property.[12]

It was always regarded as an anomaly for monks to be engaged in parish work, although in some cases permission was granted to them to do so. During the middle ages in England it was very exceptional that either the Black or White Monks did parochial work. The Canons Regular, who were not monks, served a large number of churches, although with them it was also rather exceptional. In a few instances they were allowed by indult to do the parochial work themselves, but, according to Edgerton Beck, during the middle ages the Canons rarely had the care of souls of the parish attached to their own conventual church when it happened to be parochial.[13] Regularly their churches were administered by a

[10] Council of Arles (1260), can. 15: "Districtius inhibemus ne religiosi in ecclesiis suis aut capellis laicos diebus Dominicis et solemnitatibus praecipuis recipiant ad divina; nec horis illis, in suis locis populo publice praedicent, quibus in paroeciis Missarum solemnia celebrantur."—Mansi, XXIII, 1010. See also Council of Buda, in Hungary (1279), can. 33—Mansi, XXIV, 285; c. 2, *de treuga et pace,* I, 9, in Extravag. com.

[11] Council of Mayence (847), can. 14: "Nullus monachorum parochias ecclesiarum accipere praesumat, sine consensu episcopi. De ipsis vero titulis in quibus constituti fuerint, rationem episcopo vel eius vicario reddant; et convocati ad synodum veniant."—Harduin, V, 11.

[12] This is the opinion of Hinschius, II, 283. See also DuCange, *Glossarium ad Scriptores Mediae et Infimae Latinitatis,* Paris, 1733, verbum *"Ecclesiae Paroeciales,"* V, 200.

[13] "Regulars and the Parochial System in Mediaeval England".—*Dublin Review,* p. 235-251, especially p. 242 for testimony cited.

vicar, to whom they were expected to supply enough income for a decent livelihood.[14]

With the development of a network of parochial organization it became increasingly difficult to divide parishes without injury to the rights of the people and the pastor of the old parish. When the payment of tithes and other fees had become a matter of obligation, any division of territory tended to be looked on with disfavor Although the Carolingian Capitularies during the first decades of the ninth century allowed the erection of new churches, they were careful to provide that the rights of the mother church be not prejudiced.[15]

Out of this situation there sprang what appears to be the first recorded law laying down the conditions to be verified before the erection of a new parish by the division of an old one. The council of Toulouse (843 or 844), obviously with timorous caution trying to tread a safe middle course between two opposite dangers, listed both the causes calling for such a division, and the checks to restrain the injudicious bishop. The canon is a rather long one. It obliges the bishop to obtain the consent of his chapter of canons; it warns both him and his people against acting on account of avarice; it tolerates the division only if it is morally impossible for many of the parishioners to come regularly to the old parish church.[16] The council of Tribur (895) in Germany specified that a new parish was only then to be erected when the place was more than four miles distant from the parochial church. But, judging

[14] C. 10, X, *de praebendis et dignitatibus,* III, 5

[15] Caroli I *Capitulare ad Salz.,* can. 3—MGH, *Leges,* ed. Pertz, I, 124; Caroli I, *Excerpt. Canon.,* c. 19—*op. cit.,* ed. Pertz, I, 190; Hludowic. et Hlothar. Capit., can. 6—*op. cit.* ed. Pertz, I, 254; Ansigisi Capit., lib. 2, 45—*op. cit.,* ed. Pertz, I, 299; Council of *Mayence* (847), can. 11—Harduin, V, 10.

[16] Can 7: ". . . si longitudo itineris, aut periculum aquae aut silvae, aut alicuius certae rationis vel necessitatis causa poposcerit; et si mulierum vel infantium, aut debilium imbecillitas ad ecclesiam principalem non possit occurrere."—MGH, *Leges,* ed. Pertz, I, 279; Harduin, IV, 1459.

from the wording of the canon, it appears that the bishop or his delegate was not yet the exclusive possessor of the power to divide the parishes in his diocese. The owner of the estate in which the church was located could still take the initiative in the transaction, and carry it through to its completion with the consent of the bishop. It was the estate owner who had built the church and who therefore chose its clerical and sacerdotal incumbents. Even though the bishop undertook to ensure the selection of morally suitable and intellectually competent candidates to fill these pastoral positions by insisting upon his previous approval of them, yet, without the good will and ratification of the owner of the church he felt powerless in law to avail himself authoritatively of the services of these clerics and priests for the formation of new and distinct parishes.[17]

In the Decretals of Gregory IX there is to be found an extremely important constitution of Pope Alexander III to the Archbishop of York, in England, written about the year 1170. This letter is not merely a permission: it is an uncompromising command to the Archbishop to establish a new church in a certain village which was so far from the parochial church that the parishioners could attend divine services only with the greatest of inconvenience, especially in the winter time. The letter therefore contains practically everything that was ordered by the Council of Toulouse,[18] but whereas the tone of the council was merely permissive, that of the pope's letter is mandatory. It includes many new elements. It takes into account the rich revenues of the old parish, which insure the mother church of sufficient revenue for the support of its minister, even without the income formerly received from the village. It deprives the incumbent pastor of the power to prevent the division. It prescribes that the ecclesiastical revenues of the village belong to the new church; furthermore, it indicates that a satisfactory endowment is being granted the new

[17] Can. 14—Mansi, XVIII A, 140.

[18] See footnote 16 above.

church. It directly authorizes the bishop—no one else—to accomplish the division.[19]

The inclusion of this particular constitution in the Decretals gives it immense importance, for it thereby becomes authentic law universally binding.

Another law of the Decretals denies to religious the right to divide their own parishes.[20]

The IV Council of Lateran (1215) commanded annual confession to be made by all the faithful to their own priest *(proprio sacerdoti)*,[21] a fact which gives evidence that the work of caring for souls must at that time have been extensively organized along parochial lines.

In examining these earliest laws, and in comparing them with the discipline that is in force today, the conclusion cannot be avoided that custom was the father of the first law. The actual existence of parishes prior to the enacting of the first extant parish laws governing their erection is an indisputable fact of history. When the first general legislation appears it is so com-

[19] "Ad audientiam nostram noveris pervenisse, quod villa, quae dicitiur H., tantum perhibetur ab ecclesia parochiali distare, ut *in* tempore hiemali, quum pluviae inundant, non possint parochiani sine magna difficultate ipsam adire, unde non valent congruo tempore ecclesiasticis officiis interesse. Quia igitur dicta ecclesia ita dicitur *in* reditibus abundare, quod praeter illius villae proventus minster illius convenienter valeat sustentationem habere, *fraternitati tuae per apostolica scripta mandamus,* quatenus, si res ita se habet, ecclesiam ibi aedifices, et in ea sacredotem, sublato appellationis obstaculo, ad praesentationem rectoris ecclesiae maioris cum canonico fudatoris assensu instituas, ad sustentationem suam eiusdem villae obventiones ecclesiasticas percepturum, providens tamen, ut competens in ea honor pro facultate loci matrici ecclesiae servetur, quod quidem fieri posse videtur, quum eiusdem villae dominus viginti acras terrae frugiferae velit ad usus sacerdotis conferre. Si vero persona matricis ecclesiae virum idoneum praesentare distulerit, vel opus illud voluerit impedire, tu nihilominus facias idem opus ad perfectionem deduci, et virum bonum appellationis cessante diffugio instituere non omittas."—c. 3, X, *de ecclesiis aedificandis vel reparandis,* III, 48.

[20] C. 10, X, *de praebendis et dignitatibus,* III, 5.

[21] Can. 21—Mansi, XXII, 1007.

plete and so satisfactory that its general outlines remain, substantially unchanged, until the present day.

Art. 2. *At the Council of Trent.*

Finding that the law of Alexander III, made universal by insertion into the Decretals,[22] still contained the best formula to guide the bishops when it became necessary to open new parishes, the Council of Trent explicitly approved of the norms laid down by the Constitution of Alexander III. The council is careful to say that the bishops in carrying out this prescription are acting as delegates of the Holy See in some cases. After reaffirming the old conditions for cutting off part of an old parish and erecting it into a new one, it adds a new prescription to what had already been said, for it grants to the priests appointed over the newly erected churches an equitable portion of the fruits in any wise belonging to the mother church. What the portion will amount to is left to the prudent judgment of the bishop. Furthermore, the bishop can compel the people to contribute whatever else is needed for the sustenance of their priest.[23]

[22] See footnote 19 above.

[23] "Episcopi, etiam tanquam apostolicae sedis delegati, in omnibus ecclesiis parochialibus vel baptismalibus, in quibus populus ita numerosus sit, ut rector non possit sufficere ecclesiasticis sacramentis ministrandis et cultui divino peragendo, cogant rectores, vel alios, ad quos pertinet, sibi tot sacerdotes ad hoc munus adiungere, quot sufficiant ad sacramenta exhibenda et cultum divinum celebrandum. In iis vero, in quibus ob locorum distantiam sive difficultatem parochiani sine magno incommodo ad percipienda sacramenta et divina officia audienda accedere non possunt, novas parochias etiam invitis rectoribus iuxta formam constitutionis Alexandri III, quae incipit: *Ad audientiam,* constituere possint. Illis autem sacerdotibus, qui de novo erunt ecclesiis noviter erectis praeficiendi, competens assignetur portio arbitrio episcopi ex fructibus ad ecclesiam matricem quomodocunque pertinentibus, et, si necesse fuerit, compellere possit populum ea subministrare, quae sufficiant ad vitam dictorum sacerdotum sustentandam quacunque reservatione generali vel speciali vel affectione super dictis ecclesiis non obstantibus. Neque huiusmodi ordinationes et erectiones possint tolli nec impediri ex quibuscunque provisionibus, etiam vigore resignationis, aut quibusvis aliis derogationibus vel suspensionibus."—Conc. Trident., sess. XXI, *de ref.,* c. 4.

But even during the latter half of the fifteenth century there were places which were still without definite territorial divisions, both in the cities and in the rural districts. The council, not satisfied to express a mere preference that such inadequate organization be made more complete, strictly commanded that parishes be established wherever possible, and that every community should have its own pastor to whom alone they should go for the lawful reception of the sacraments. Definite boundaries were to be set for all parishes.[24]

Art. 3. *After the Council of Trent.*

From the tenor of subsequent legislation it can be seen that all the influence of the Council of Trent was not able to bring about an immediate reform in the lax and incomplete organization that had prevailed in many places. A century and a half after the council Innocent III [25] and Benedict XIV [26] found it necessary to remind the bishops that the law of Trent had not lost any of its force.

The law of the Council of Trent remained the norm for the universal Church up to the time of the Code. The S. Congregation of the Council was called upon frequently to interpret the law, and the Rota decided questions of fact, but their decisions and sentences merely helped to clarify difficulties and to crystallize the practice of the Church along more or less stable lines. As is to be seen in the commentary, most of the regulations of the

[24] ". . . In iis quoque civitatibus ac locis, ubi parochiales ecclesiae certos non habent fines, nec earum rectores proprium populum, quem regant, sed promiscue pententibus sacramenta administrant, mandat sancta synodus episcopis pro tutiori animarum eis commissarum salute, ut distincto populo in certas propriasque parochias unicuique suum perpetuum peculiaremque parochum assignent, qui eas cognoscere valeat, et a quo solo licite sacramenta suscipiant. aut alio utiliori modo, prout loci qualitas exegerit, provideant. Idemque in iis civitatibus ac locis, ubi nullae sunt parochiales, quamprimum fieri curent, non obstantibus quibuscunque privilegiis ac consuetudinibus, etiam immemorabilibus."—Council of Trent, sess, XXIV, *de ref.*, c. 13.

[25] Const. "*Apostolici ministerii*", Mai. 23,1723, n. 14—*Fontes,* n. 280.

[26] Const. "Ad militantis", Mar. 30, 1742, nn. 11 and 16—*Fontes, n. 326.*

old law have been perpetuated in the Code. Consequently to evaluate the importance and trend of the interpretations and practice of the Holy See pertains to the Commentary that follows because they are frequently the basis of interpretation for the present law.

Section IV. Summary.

The constitution of the Church does not prescribe any juridical division of the faithful among pastors of less than episcopal rank. The plan followed by the Apostles in caring for their many converts was simply to consecrate bishops in the larger cities, conferring on them the power to ordain other priests as their helpers. The opening of a church at a distance from the city implied the consecrating of another bishop. Such churches were not established in country districts. From sources at hand it seems safe to conclude that throughout the first two centuries these priests lived a sort of community life under the supervision of their bishop, acting as his personal delegates among the faithful of the city and of the immediate vicinity.

When, about the beginning of the fourth century, the great increase in the number of the faithful made it impossible for the bishop to function efficiently as the only pastoral official in his territory, priests began to receive a share of responsibility in certain parts of the diocese, and by degrees the faculties to administer the sacraments and to say Mass away from the cathedral.

The earliest signs of parochial innovation are to be found in the Orient. There the *chorepiscopi,* or land-bishops of the third and fourth century, were probably the first pastors, for they did exercise some jurisdiction outside of the episcopal cities, although they remained subject to their respective urban bishops. Too little information can be gleaned from the sources to say definitely what specific functions they exercised, but it seems certain that they had some limited jurisdiction over the people in the vicinity, and over a body of priests who lived a sort of community life as the assistants of the *chorepiscopi*. Resident *chorepiscopi* in time gave way to priests in village and country districts.

As early as the end of the fourth century there were extra-urban churches in the suburbs of Alexandria in charge of resident priests who were not *chorepiscopi.* Still, the nature of the pastoral office of these priests remains obscure.

At the council of Nicea in 787 it was decreed that permanent residence must be maintained by clerics at the churches for which they were ordained.

The city of Rome very probably had parishes long before any other city of the West. Before the end of the persecutions the Eternal City had been divided into *tituli,* which were assigned to priests who exercised therein many of the functions of modern parish priests, but without the right to say Mass on Sundays and on certain feast days.

Not before the beginning of the fourth century is there evidence of parish churches in the West outside of Rome, but about that time they begin to develop simultaneously in Spain and France, and a little later in Italy and Africa.

The most striking characteristic of the parish legislation of this period was the emphasis placed on permanent residence at the church for which one was ordained, in order to insure adequate ministrations for the parishioners. It was recommended that assistant priests be obtained to supply for unavoidable absence on the part of the pastor, and even deacons were to be used in an emergency, to read from a homily of the Fathers

By the end of the eighth century parochial legislation of the East and West had reached practically the same stage of development.

Until the year 1000 there were no city parishes outside of Rome and Alexandria, and even when they began to appear in episcopal cities their status remained obscure. Their boundaries were vague; their functions were poorly defined; their very existence was not universal until after the Council of Trent.

Oratories on private estates and in monasteries often obtained a parochial status when their incumbents were granted faculties to administer the sacraments to people within certain territorial limits. The councils opposed the usurpation by oratories of parochial duties without permission of the bishop.

The first positive law on record regarding the establishing of new parishes by division was enacted by the council of Toulouse in the year 843 or 844 in which the necessity of dividing parishes for the good of souls was recognized, and at the same time checks were enumerated to prevent too hasty action on the part of bishops. Other councils point out the reasons justifying division of older parishes and indicate the manner in which it is to be accomplished.

When the good of souls calls for the erection of another parish, there is an obligation, not merely a permission, for the bishop to accomplish the founding, according to the law of the Decretals of Gregory IX, which gives universal binding force to a particular constitution of Alexander III. Decretal law laid down practically the same rules that still bind today.

The Council of Trent added little new law to that of the Decretals, because that law was already satisfactory. The council simply endeavored to see that the law was more universally adopted and obeyed.

The Holy See has been concerned since that time with the application of the law to particular cases, not with the enactment of new laws.

CHAPTER III

PRELIMINARY NOTIONS CONCERNING PROCEDURE

Art. 1. *Legal Nature of Parishes*

In order to avoid confusion in the use of terms in the pages to follow, a brief discussion of the legal nature of parishes will be useful. Parishes are a species of benefices. Legislation that is specifically parochial is to be found in Book III of the Code, title XXV, which is devoted to the regulations regarding benefices. According to canon 1409 an ecclesiastical benefice is a juridic entity which has been permanently established or erected by a competent ecclesiastical authority, and which consists of a sacred office and of the right to receive the revenue from the funds attached to the office.

a) A juridic entity is synonymous with a moral person.[1] An ecclesiastical benefice, therefore, is a moral, not a physical person; in other words, although it is not a physical person, yet it is something which by a fiction of law is accredited as capable of enjoying rights and of owing obligations. It is non-collegiate, because it is made up of a sacred office and of the right to revenue, rather than of the several physical persons which are necessary for the erection of a collegiate moral person.[2]

b) A benefice is constituted by a competent ecclesiastical authority. The Catholic Church and the Apostolic See alone hold their legal personality by divine institution. All other ecclesiastical moral persons, because they contain a supernatural element, viz., a sacred office, which cannot be conferred by any purely human institution, must derive their legal personality from God through His Church. The Supreme Pontiff who holds supreme jurisdiction in the Church alone possesses immediately the power

[1] Coronata, *Institutiones,* I, n. 135.

[2] Canons 99 and 100, § 2.

to establish subordinate ecclesiastical moral persons; and he can exercise it directly, by his own act, or indirectly, through other persons, either physical or moral, whom he delegates, or to whom he gives ordinary power. Some moral persons in the Church, for instance the Sacred College of Cardinals, owe their legal personality to the general law; others, including dioceses and parishes, are generated by a particular decree of a competent superior. The civil authority has no power whatsoever to erect ecclesiastical benefices even when, by concordats, it has the right to approve the erection of parishes, because the state can never have jurisdiction over any effects except those that are civil.[3]

c) The erection must be in perpetuity. Of its nature a benefice must be permanent, because all juridical entities must of their nature be permanent. It cannot cease to exist of its own accord, but only because a lawful external authority acting through positive law or by particular decree is responsible for its dissolution.[4]

The tenure of the incumbent of the benefice may be temporary, or removable; or it may be permanent, or irremovable. [5] In either case whenever the office for any reason becomes vacant it is understood that another beneficiary must be appointed to fill the benefice which continues in its existence.

d) A benefice must be established or erected. A formal decree of the competent superior is required. This question will be discussed in detail later.

e) A benefice consists of a sacred office. The Code defines *sacred office*, in a strict sense, as "an ecclesiastical function of a permanent character established by divine or ecclesiastical authority, to be conferred in accordance with the rules laid down in the sacred canons and implying at least some participation of ecclesiastical power, either of orders or of jurisdiction". This strict sense applies to benefices.[6]

[3] Coronata, *Institutiones,* II, n. 972, I. An example can be found in the Concordat of 1801 with France, Art IX—Nussi, *Conventiones inter S. Sedem et Civilem Potestatem,* p. 139.

[4] Can. 102, § 1.

[5] Pistocchi, *De Re Beneficiali,* p. 9; Coronata, *Institutiones,* II, n. 972, I.

[6] Can. 145, §§ 1 and 2.

f) The right of the incumbent to receive the revenue from the funds attached to the office normally implies the existence of an endowment as an essential property of a benefice. Formerly endowment consisted of land or real estate. The present law accepts as endowments not only the goods belonging to the juridical being, but also definite contributions to be given by a family or moral person, definite and voluntary offerings of the faithful which accrue to the rector of the benefice, stole fees within the limit set by diocesan statute or legitimate custom, and choir distributions in chapters.[7]

Art. 2. *Methods of Erecting Parishes*

As has been noted in the historical section of this work, the Church did not by general legislation originate the territorial organization by means of which she has functioned for many centuries. Rather her legislation was but the recognition and regulation of an accomplished fact. It is very significant that the first universal law dealing with parish organization refers to the division of units that already existed. The constitution *"Ad audientiam"* of Alexander III (ca. 1170), which was incorporated into the Decretals and specifically approved by the Council of Trent, is concerned with division. It is noteworthy that such a fundamental institution could have been taken for granted for so many centuries before the Council of Trent[8] drew up the first law which made obligatory the creation of parishes in districts where none existed, and which so precisely defined the constitutive elements that those elements have remained without essential change or substantial addition even after the Code.[9]

Parishes Erected by Way of Creation

There are actually only two modes of erecting new parishes, namely, by creation and by division. Erection by creation takes

[7] Can. 1410.

[8] Sess. XXIV, *de ref.*, c. 13.

[9] For texts of these laws and discussion see preceding chapter.

place when a previously undivided diocese or its equivalent is subdivided for the first time, so that from a territory and people previously assigned to no parish a new parish is established. There can be no doubt about the obligation of the bishop of a diocese which is subject to the prescriptions of the Code to see that his entire diocese is divided according to the prescriptions of canon 216, § 1. Because such territorial parochial division is not something new with the Code, but has been mandatory since the Council of Trent,[10] undivided dioceses are extremely rare today. With the exception of the unique historical realignment of parishes in France in 1801, when Pope Pius VII in a concordat with Napoleon entirely suppressed all previously existing parishes and created new ones,[11] creation is very uncommon in recent times except in the missions.

Creation is, however, a quite common and often perplexing problem in dioceses subject to the S. Congregation of the Propagation of the Faith and in vicariates and prefectures apostolic. While canon 216, § 2, orders that the prescriptions of canon 216, § 1, be put into effect in prefectures and vicariates apostolic, it adds the clause "insofar as it is practicable". Obviously, in the missions the means are not always at hand to staff and support and conduct a complete parochial or quasi-parochial organization. The problem is not one of law but of expediency, because there the law explicitly yields to unfavorable circumstances. Supplementing the law of the Code is an instruction which urges that such division of the territory of vicariates apostolic, and prefectures apostolic be prepared for and made as soon as possible, but cautions also that it should not be made prematurely. The norm should be the welfare of souls and the good of the Church. If the time is not opportune to divide the whole prefecture or vicariate, various parts can be erected into quasi-parishes as suitable opportunity presents itself, the remaining territory being left unchanged. The judgment as to whether the division is not only possible, but also sound from an

[10] Sess. XXIV, *de ref.*, c. 13; Benedict XIV, const. "*Ad militantis*", Mar. 30, 1742, n. 16—*Fontes*, n. 326.

[11] Nussi, *Conventiones inter S. Sedem et Civilem Potestatem*, p. 139.

administrative viewpoint, is left to the ordinary after he consults his advisors according to canon 302.[12] A similar concession was extended to missionary dioceses subject to the S. Congregation of the Propagation of the Faith where the same problems are present.[13] Consequently erection by creation could also take place in a district where the previous subdivision had been only partially accomplished, or where the earlier boundaries are too vague or doubtful.[14]

Parishes Erected by Way of Division

Whereas creation is the method of erecting parishes in virgin territory, division is the method to be used in places where parishes already exist. Division is the method by which one or several new parishes are established in territory that previously belonged to one or more older parishes. At least one new juridic entiry, one new moral person, is thereby brought into being. Division should be carefully distinguished from dismemberment, because the definition of these terms in canon 1421 has practically, but not entirely, put an end to the indiscriminate use made of them previously. Although they are interchanged in canon 1500 the reversed meaning is not used anywhere else in the Code. Dismemberment now signifies not the same thing as division, but rather the transferring of part of the territory or goods of one parish to another already existing parish without the establishment of a new parish. Because dismemberment does not give rise to a new moral person, it is not to be considered in this work as a method of erecting a parish. Until the Code became effective the word *dismemberment* was widely used, even in official sources, as a synonym for division.[15]

[12] S. C. Prop. Fid., instr., July 25, 1920, n. 1—AAS, XII (1920), 331.

[13] S. C. Prop. Fid., decr., Dec. 9, 1920, n. 1—AAS, XIII (1921), 17.

[14] Maroto, *Institutiones*, II, n. 771.

[15] See the index to almost any volume of AAS, as late as vol. IX (1917), e.g., pp. 509-516. See pre-Code *Rota Decisions* and the *Thesaurus Resolutionum S. C. Concilii.* Authors as a rule followed the terminology used in official sources. See Bouix, *De Parocho*, p. 242. On the other hand Ojetti, in his *Synopsis* (which was published in 1899, page 146) defines division and dismemberment in the same way as the Code does.

CHAPTER IV

CONDITIONS FOR THE ERECTION OF PARISHES

Art. 1. *Competent Authority*

The Holy See enjoys unrestricted competence for the erection of any kind of parishes. The local ordinary possesses a more restricted competence. Since the Code has become the common and universal law of the Church his legal right and competence to divide parishes rest fully upon one basis—his ordinary powers of office. Formerly, in view of the two sources from which a local ordinary derived his competence in this matter, he could function with delegated as well as ordinary power. The decree of Alexander III, *"Ad audientiam,"* which still remains substantially unchanged, granted ordinary power.[1] The Council of Trent provided him also with delegated power over "all parochial and baptismal churches," for it authorized the bishops of dioceses to act *etiam tamquam Apostolicae Sedis delegati.* This delegated authority was granted by the Holy See in order that bishops might have the right to proceed against the parishes which were held by exempt religious and which were immediately subject to the Holy See. The right of this exemption was not violated by the bishops when they acted in the capacity of delegates of the Apostolic See. The word *etiam* in the concession made by the Council implies that the grant of delegated power extended also to the division of parishes over which the bishop already possesed ordinary power. Consequently, in circumstances where he possessed double power he could exercise either.[2]

Canon 1414, § 2, states that the local ordinary (as defined in canon 198, § 2), in his own territory can erect non-consistorial benefices. Parishes are non-consistorial benefices. However, para-

[1] C. 3, X, *de ecclesiis aedificandis vel reparandis,* III, 48.

[2] Cf. Bouix, *De Parocho,* p. 246-248, 279. Cf. also, "De potestate Ordinariorum, deque iurisprudentia quoad Paroeciarum dismembrationem," ASS, XIII (1880), appendix VI, p. 299-307.

graph 3 of the same canon denies competence to the vicar general unless he has a special mandate. Canon 1427 then gives more specific rules for the erection of parochial benefices by division.

But can the ordinary who administers a diocese during the vacancy of the see, namely, the cathedral chapter or the vicar capitular or the administrator, validly or licitly erect new parishes? If it is a question of creating a new parish from new territory there is no law of the Code forbidding it. It seems lawful, according to canon 1414. But the question of the dividing of parishes by the vicar capitular is a more difficult one. It is not evident from the text of the law that he does not have the power given to ordinaries by canon 1427, §1. The presumption should favor him until the contrary is proved, because in the very definition of ordinary in canon 198 the Code states that: "in law, by the name of ordinary are to be understood, unless a contrary exception is expressly made . . . those who fill the place when there is no residential bishop . . ." Nowhere in the Code is the vicar capitular or the cathedral chapter expressly forbidden to divide parishes. Some canonists see such a prohibition in the possible extension of the wording of canon 1423, § 1, which does expressly deny him the power to unite parishes.[3] It is hard to see why the legislator should grant the vicar capitular the right to erect new parishes by division, while denying him the right to unite parishes, but if the legislator intended the restriction to apply in both cases, why did he not make the restriction equally apparent in both cases?

Augustine points to canon 436, *"sede vacante nihil innovetur,"* as an additional reason why the vicar capitular should be considered incompetent in this matter.[4] The usual interpretation of

[3] Vermeersch-Creusen (*Epitome,* II, 532), deny the power of the vicar capitular "on account of the analogy drawn from can. 1423." See also Augustine, *Canonical and Civil Status of Catholic Parishes in the United States,* p. 157; Ayrinhac, *Administrative Legislation,* p. 325. On the other hand, Rossi (*De Paroecia,* p. 21) indicates that the vicar capitular does possess this power from can. 1414, § 3.

[4] *Canonical and Civil Status of Catholic Parishes,* p. 157. However, in his *Commentary* (II, 489) Augustine does not include the erection of parishes in his list of functions forbidden to vicars capitular, nor does Coronata. Cf.

canon 436, however, is built on an analogy by which the relationship between vicar and diocese is compared to that which exists between tutor and ward: the vicar must not undertake anything which will substantially harm his diocese or the rights of the next bishop, but he may conduct business that will accrue to the benefit of the diocese.[5] Thus, if he foresees that the proposed division of a parish, which is in fact a substantial portion of the diocese, will not only not be harmful, but even directly beneficial to the diocese, canon 436 will not of itself prevent the making of such a division. Thus, it might happen that the grave necessity of providing more adequate care for souls in a rapidly growing district is too urgent to be postponed until the next bishop arrives.

An apostolic administrator permanently appointed enjoys the same power as a residential bishop. If he is only temporarily appointed he has the same power as a vicar capitular.[6]

The case against the power of the vicar capitular, therefore, does not seem to be impenetrable, for the reasons proposed. Perhaps an objection against his competence might be drawn from the fact that he cannot validly *confer* a parish until a year after the diocese has become vacant.[7] If he cannot appoint a permanent "proprius sacerdos" within a year, the territorial division that he would erect would lack temporarily one of the elements essential to a parish in its normal condition. The objection does not have great weight, because the actual incumbency of a permanent pastor is not necessary for the existence of the parochial moral person. Nor would the difficulty last after the diocese has been vacant a year.

In view of the negative opinion of most canonists who have mentioned the problem it would seem unwise for the vicar capitular or administrator to proceed to a new foundation, unless the needs of the people are too urgent to brook delay. But if the vicar

Institutiones, I, n. 461. Cf. also Jaeger, *The Administration of Vacant and Quasi-vacant Dioceses in the United States,* p. 190 and 195.

[5] Coronata, *Institutiones,* I, n. 461; Vermeersch-Creusen, *Epitome,* I, n. 527; Jaeger, *op. cit.,* p. 190.

[6] Can. 315, § 1 and 2. In the United States there are no cathedral chapters. The consultors elect an administrator who is equivalent to a vicar capitular.

[7] Can. 455, § 2, 3°.

capitular or administrator establishes a new parish when all other conditions are verified, the division might be upheld by the Sacred Congregation of the Council.

For a discussion of the competence of the local ordinary to change the status of so-called religious parishes and of parishes serving special groups see Chapter VI of this work.

Art. 2. *Canonical Cause*

Canon 1427, § 2.—Causa canonica ut divisio aut dismembratio paroeciae fieri possit, ea tantum est, si aut magna sit difficultas accedendi ad ecclesiam paroecialem, aut nimia sit paroecianorum multitudo, quorum bono spirituali subveniri nequeat ad normam can. 476, § 1.

Canon 1428, § 2.—Unio, translatio, divisio, dismembratio facta sine canonica causa irrita est.

It is scarcely proper to speak of a canonical cause being present to justify the creation of a new parish where no parish existed previously. If the parochial subdivision of a diocese is possible and feasible from an administrative viewpoint the subdivision is obligatory without further consideration of cause.

On the other hand, the division of a benefice, including a parochial benefice, has always been considered to be something odious because it involves the deprivation of certain spiritual and temporal rights.[8] In some countries where the population is stable and of meager financial means the income of the clergy in regularly established parishes is barely sufficient to meet necessary expenses. Any part of their territory that is cut off means the irremediable loss of certain contributions from part of the inhabi-

[8] Abbas Panormitanus (Nicholaus de Tudeschis, d. 1445) wrote in the XV century "Non enim debet sine causa parochia ecclesiae dividi. Est enim ista alienatio iurium ecclesiae quae sine causa fieri non debet."—*Lectura in Lib. III Decretalium*, cap. 3, tit. 48, n. 2. See also S. C. C., *Dismembrationis*, Sept. 16, 1871—ASS, VII (1872), 41. In the same vein Card. De Luca wrote: "Per erectionem (novae) depauperetur antiqua ecclesia paroecialis, eiusque dignitas vilesceret"—*De Decimis*, disc. 12, n. 8.

tants—irrevocable because there is no prospect of growth of population by immigation. That objection is not so important in countries where the population is growing rapidly. Division does, however, always involve the loss of jurisdiction by the pastor over part of his former subjects. The legislator is so reluctant to deprive a beneficiary of acquired rights that he forbids the division of parishes without a canonical cause under pain of nullity, and he limits the valid causes to two, namely, great difficulty for a notable number of parishioners to attend the parish church, and an excessive number of parishioners.

DIFFICULTY FOR PARISHIONERS TO ATTEND

Although the law governing difficulty of approach as a canonical cause has remained the same ever since the Council of Trent, the interpretation of the law has undergone certain substantial changes. Formerly the division of a parish was considered an extraordinary remedy for the deficient care of the spiritual needs of the people. The one cause for which the Council allows division is that the parishioners be otherwise unable to reach the church without great inconvenience *(magnum incommodum)*. Furthermore, even in that case, if the needs of the people could be attended by the appointment of extra curates, or even by assigning priests to dependent chapels without parochial rights, division was forbidden.[9]

Cardinal De Luca (1614-1683), who himself was an advocate of the Rota, points out that, in the matter of division of parishes by the bishop, a sure general norm adaptable to every possible case without exception cannot be defined. Therefore, it is an error to adopt as a general rule for all cases a particular declaration of the Sacred Congregation, or a decision of the Rota, or an opinion of canonists in permitting or denying a new erection of a parish since each case must be decided on its own merits. While, for instance, distance and difficulty of approach may be the same in two instances, the new foundation may be justified in one case by cir-

[9] Council of Trent, sess. XXI, *de ref.*, c. 4.

cumstances which are lacking in the other. The general rule is that division is forbidden as an odious alienation if the needs of the people can be administered to by assistant priests.[10]

Fagnanus seemed to favor a not too strict interpretation, because he did not demand moral impossibility for the parishioners to attend divine services. He quotes with approval the statement of Nepos: "illud solum possumus quod commode possumus."[11]

For two centuries canonical practice followed a rigorous interpretation of the Council. Rota decisions during those centuries constantly refused to permit division, except as an extreme remedy, when adjutants or assistant priests would suffice.[12]

About the middle of the XVIII Century, with a change in the economic and social and religious conditions of the people, the "great inconvenience" demanded by the Council began to receive a milder interpretation.[13] The trend of interpretation toward mildness is evident from the decision of the Sacred Congregation of the Council made in 1879, in which it is pointed out that the supreme law in this matter is the salvation of souls, and that pastors are given to the people, not the people to the pastors. In

[10] *Adnotationes ad S. Conc. Trid.*, disc. 16, nn. 1 and 3.

[11] *Commentarium in Decretalium*, lib. III, tit. 48, c. 3, n. 2.

[12] S. R. Rota, *Oveten.*, May 12, 1681—*Decisiones*, 578, part. 19, tome II, *recent.*, n. 8, p. 470. "Domini, praesupposita etiam subsistentia causarum, eas non sufficere crediderunt quotiescumque potest aliunde provideri cum dismembratio sit remedium extraordinarium et subsidiarium, ad quod numquam a Iudicibus devenire solet, quotiescumque adsit aliud remedium minis odiosum, et exorbitans."—S. R. Rota, *Leodien. Dismembrationis*, Feb. 1, 1712,—*Coram Falconerio*, Vol. IV, decis. 34, p. 79. See also S. C. C., *Lunen. Sarazen., Dismembrationis paroeciae*, Sept. 27, 1732—*Thes. Res.*, V (1730-1732), 376. S. C. C., *Cassanen.*, Dec. 17, 1740, declared null a division which could have been avoided by appointing curates.—*Thes. Res.*, IX (1739-40), 101 secundo.

[13] "Censuit enim deveniendum esse ad dismembrationem paroeciae, tametsi rector veteris parochiae retinere offerret in aliqua cappella cappellanum qui occurrere valeret spiritualibus indigentiis parochianorum, qui iusta de causa instabant pro dismembratione." This passage is cited from S. C. C. *Comen.*, Dec. 3, 1750 in S. R. Rota, *Lucana*, Apr. 23, 1917—AAS, IX (1917), p. 511. See also S. C. C., *Reatina*, Sept. 20, 1817—*Thes. Res.*, LXXVII (1817), 286

the case which was decided in favor of division the people were being given satisfactory administration by curates who were stationed at outlying chapels. However, it was argued with telling effect before the sacred congregation that the great distance from the parish church, and the hardships of travel, made it necessary to attend the chapels exclusively, and therefore deprived the very young and the very old, the weak, and women, of the opportunity of ever hearing the voice of their own pastor and of ever approaching him, or of ever attending the parish church.[14]

In the remarks which follow that decision the commentator indicates that in recent juridical practice division was no longer considered an extreme remedy, if it was evidently useful for the good of souls and at the same time there was sufficient revenue to support both the new and the old parishes. He points out further that, if a useful division has been made, the Sacred Congregation of the Council is inclined to support the act of the bishop even if certain formalities of the process have not been complied with. The opinion of the commentator is not new. It agrees with the comment on an earlier decision.[15]

In a decision rendered a few years before the publication of the Code the Rota was even more liberal. "Note," it says, "that nowadays dismemberment (division) is to be made more easily, and is no longer to be considered, as it was formerly, an extreme remedy not to be applied when the care of souls could be provided otherwise, for instance, by a vicar. The reason for this milder practice is that today the lax morals of youth and the devastating

[14] S. C. C., *Scarmagno,* Sept. 29, 1879—ASS, XIII (1880), 279. See also Rucupis, "The Canonical Formation of Parishes and Missions," *American Eccles. Review,* LV (1916), 238-250, esp. p. 242.

[15] ASS, XIII (1880), 307; and VII (1872), 45, footnote. The older practice of preferring to serve the people by means of chaplains removable *ad nutum episcopi* in outlying succursal churches does not appear to be in harmony with the law of the Council of Trent that "distincto populo in certas propriasque parochias suum perpetuum peculiaremque parochum assignent, qui eas cognoscere valeat, et a quo solo licite sacramenta recipiant" (sess. XXIV, *de ref.* c. 13), as was pointed out in S. C. C., *Concordien.,* Jan. 19, 1889—ASS, XXII (1889), 74.

inroads of masonic sects which prowl about like hungry wolves seeking to devour the flock of Christ, indicate at least the evident utility, if not the absolute necessity, of multiplying shepherds. Among the shepherds everybody realizes that true pastors are to be preferred to vicars."[16] This is the evident utility of which Sebastianelli writes when he says that "a just cause is moral necessity and the evident utility of the church which should be such that the church in whose favor the dismemberment (division) is made cannot otherwise be adequately provided.[17]

Another factor which was admitted by the Rota as a supplementary cause to justify division is violent antipathy which, though blameworthy, nevertheless hinders a notable part of the people from being ruled by one pastor in the amicable manner productive of spiritual good.[18]

The Code put a sudden end to the trend towards laxity by recognizing as the sole canonical causes for division of a parish great difficulty for the people to approach the parish church, or a multitude of parishioners so numerous that their spiritual needs cannot be supplied even by the help of assistants. The Code therefore restricts the tendency toward giving the force of a canonical cause to what actually is only an aggravating circumstance. Thus, dissention among the parishioners, no matter how bitter, is no longer of itself sufficient cause. Nor is the cause of simple utility enough, if it merely makes more convenient what was already not very difficult.[19]

[16] S. R. Rota, *Sedunen.* Apr. 2, 1912—AAS, IV. (1912), 454; *Decisiones,* IV (1912), 154, n. 4.

[17] *Praelectiones I. C., De Rebus,* p. 326. Utility is not a new cause; De Luca speaks of "justa causa necessitatis vel utilitatis" in *De Regular.,* disc. 5, n. 4. Bouix *(De Parocho,* p. 250) quotes the secretary of the S. C. Council in the case of *Massanen.,* May 9, 1840, as approving evident utility of the church as a cause.

[18] S. R. Rota, *Bobien.,* Mar. 4, 1911—*Decisiones coram Lega,* dec. III, n. 2, p. 166; *Sedunen.,* Apr. 2, 1912—AAS, IV (1912), 454, *S. R. Rotae Decisiones,* IV (1912), 153, n. 4; *Lucana,* Apr. 23, 1917—AAS, IX (1917), 509; S. C. C., *Concordien.,* Jan. 19, 1889—ASS, XXII (1889), 73.

[19] Pistocchi, *De Re Beneficiali,* p. 117.

Great difficulty for the people to go to the parish church may arise from any cause, and it does not mean a very great difficulty. The word used is *magna,* not *maxima.* Ayrinhac cautiously states that the difficulty perhaps does not have to be objectively and in itself really great, as long as it proves so subjectively, and does in practice prevent a notable number of the faithful from going to the parish church for mass and the sacraments.[20] The ordinary would seem to be justified in attaching considerable importance to the opinion of Ayrinhac, since the division of a parish is a question rather of fact than of law. Since, therefore, the final decision rests upon the valuation which the ordinary puts upon the facts rather than upon any inflexible precedents, in estimating the magnitude of the difficulty of approach the common consensus of opinion of the inhabitants is a helpful norm for applying the law in particular cases.[21]

The source of the difficulty is twofold. It may be the distance which the people must travel in order to reach the church[22] or it may be the difficulties and obstacles encountered on the way.[23] In either case, it is only when the distance or the obstacles to travel give rise to great difficulty that there is present a canonical cause for valid and licit division. Although relatively slight inconvenience will not suffice as a cause, yet it does suffice that the old parish be so extensive that the people, especially in unfavorable weather, find it very difficult to gather at a precise time for divine services. In these days, when mechanical conveyances make possible quicker and more accurately scheduled travel, many people do not find serious difficulty in traveling much greater distances than were indicated during preceding centuries. Nevertheless, even in prosperous times a large proportion of the people cannot afford to travel by public or private conveyance without "great hardship."

Great distance, not being in itself a cause for division, but merely

[20] *Administrative Legislation,* p. 326.

[21] De Luca, *De Decimis,* disc. 12, n. 9, and *Adnotationes ad S. Conc. Tria.,* disc. 16, n. 1 and 2.

[22] C. 3, X, *de ecclesiis aedificandis vel reparandis,* III, 48.

[23] Conc. Trident., sess. XXI, *de ref.* c. 4.

a source of great inconvenience, has not been defined by law, but is to be determined by the ordinary. It is usually considered to be a cause of grave inconvenience when it amounts to about 2000 *passus,* or two Roman miles, which are equivalent to about 1¾ English statute miles.[24] The practice of the Roman tribunals has been to uphold divisions made by the bishop when a notable portion of the people resided two miles from the parish church, and to reverse the order of the bishop when the distance was less than 1½ miles.[25]

It is obvious that physical obstacles in the road may render the approach to the church not only very difficult, but even dangerous. Akin to the precipitous paths, slippery roads, unbridged streams and other similar natural hindrances, obstructions and hazards, and also the lengthy permanent detours on which the S. Congregation of the Council based many of its decisions[26] are our modern busy and perilous railroad grade crossings and express highways, especially where there are many children. Any of these reasons by itself is sufficient to supply a canonical cause, even though the distance to be traversed may be much less than a mile.

The Code does not renew the old prescriptions about avoiding division by appointing curates in outlying dependent chapels to care for those who are prevented by extrinsic reasons from attending the parish church, provided, of course, that all other qualities necessary in a new parish are present. Canon 476, which prescribes the appointment of curates, places the good of souls in the place of first importance.[27]

[24] The Ancient Roman mile was about 1620 English yards (1428 meters). The English statute mile used in Great Britain, the United States, etc., is equal to 1760 yards (1609 meters)—*Webster's Collegiate Dictionary,* Springfield, 1936.

[25] S. R. Rota, *Sedunen.,* Apr. 2, 1912—*Decisiones,* IV (1909), 154; S. C. C. *Placentina,* May 28, 1791—*Thes. Resol.,* LX (1791), 136; *Aquen.,* Aug. 2, 1721—*Thes. Resol.,* II (1721-1723), 56. See also Bouix, *De Parocho,* p. 263.

[26] Bouix, *De Parocho,* p. 258; Barbosa, *Collect. Doct. in Conc. Trid.,* sess. XXI, *de ref.,* c. 4, n. 6-11.

[27] Can. 476, § 8.

EXCESSIVE NUMBER OF PARISHIONERS

On the other cause admitted by canon 1427, § 2, namely an excessive number of parishioners, the legislator places a restriction. If, by receiving one or more assistant priests to help him, the pastor can render satisfactory care to the spiritual needs of his large flock, this cause for division of the parish vanishes.[28] It is true that the excessive population of certain parishes was proposed to the Roman tribunals as a reason for division, but the cases, which were infrequent, were usually supported by other reasons. In itself, this cause was rejected by the old law.[29]

There has been no official universal declaration from the Holy See defining the maximum population to be allowed in any parish. In fact, the official pronouncements in particular cases are so widely divergent as to be of no value as a general norm. Pius VI, in the brief *"Quod aliquantum"* addressed to the bishops of France (March 10, 1791), clearly disapproved of the practice of having as many as six thousand parishioners in one parish in Paris.[30] Whether or not the pastors had assistant priests to aid them is not discussed by the Pope, and consequently the text seems to reflect his mind towards all cases. On the other hand, the S. C. of the Council seemed not to be surprised to find a pastor having recourse against a decree of his ordinary when the latter had divided the parish for the sole reason that it contained as many as 32,000 souls. The pastor maintained that with the aid of his fifteen curates he was capable of giving adequate care to all! The decree of the bishop was sustained.[31] The problem is confused by another case in which the Congregation thought it unwise to divide a parish in the care of the Capuchins, chiefly on the grounds that the popula-

[28] Can. 476, § 1.

[29] Fagnanus, *Commentarium* in Lib. III, tit. 48, c. 3, n. 24.

[30] This constitution is not found in the *Fontes* or the *Bullarium*. Ayrinhac refers to it in *"Administrative Legislation in the New Code of Canon Law,"* p. 326 under the name *"Aliquantulum."*

[31] S. C. C., *Syracusana*, Mar. 28, 1903—*Fontes*, n. 4313.

tion had increased to 6500. Two years later, owing to a further rapid increase in population, the division was allowed.[32]

Again, as in every other question of fact regarding the causes, the decision as to the existence or non-existence of the cause is left to the judgment of the ordinary, who must rely on precedent and on his own prudence for guidance in particular cases. He is to base his decision on such considerations as these: For instance, the number might exceed the capacity of the permanent church which was constructed to accommodate a smaller congregation; or a zealous pastor might find it impossible to render the reasonable, personal services which are expected of him and to attend to the reasonable requests of his too numerous flock. He would not be able to "know his sheep." Modern authors suggest 6000 as being probably more parishioners than one pastor in a typical parish can care for even with the help of assistants.[33]

Any one canonical cause alone—no matter what be the source of it, whether it be due to distance, or physical obstacles or hazards, or whether it be due to excessive population—is sufficient to make lawful the division. It is not necessary that both great difficulty of approach and excessive population concur simultaneously. If both causes are present, but only in a partial degree, so that the bishop might remain doubtful about the sufficiency of either of the two causes singly, the cumulative effects in many cases could well be such as to justify fully the issuing of the contemplated decree.

Art. 3. *Sufficient Population*

The Code does not touch the problem of the minimum number of people for whom a parish may be erected. The *populus determinatus* to be assigned to a territorial division of a diocese according to canon 216, § 1, can only be determined from the pre-Code practice. The Code literally adopts the phrase from the Council

[32] S. C. C., *Taurin.*, Jan. 21, 1905 and July 27, 1907—*Fontes* nn. 4320 and 4339.

[33] Coronata, *Institutiones*, II, n. 983, p. 379.

of Trent, which was no more specific than the Code is.[34] Canonists obtain a certain precarious legal footing for their opinions from the very early laws of the Church. The Decree of Gratian contains a canon which permits the appointment of a priest over a church which has at least ten *mancipia,*[35] a canon which was taken from the XVI Council of Toledo (731).[36] It is inconceivable that this council could have been speaking of the term in its classical signification, of slaves.[37]

Some of the earlier canonists defended the theory that the *mancipia* used in the law of Gratian meant single persons. The Glossator apparently held that opinion, although it is not indisputably clear from the short text. Again, in the gloss to c. 1, X, *de electione et electi potestate,* I, 6, *populus* is described as ten persons. Fagnanus argues that since *populus* and *decem mancipia* are synonymous, and since *populus* means ten individuals, then *decem mancipia* also means ten individuals.[38]

"Mancipia" has been more commonly interpreted by canonists as meaning families. Corradus held that if ten persons remained they constituted a sufficient population for a parish, but according to his context he clearly means that ten persons suffice to maintain an already existing parish. Where it is a question of erecting a new parish, he thinks with the Rota that three homes with fifteen constituents, or even five homes with twenty constituents, is scarcely a sufficient population.[39]

[34] Sess. XXIV, *de ref.,* c. 13; sess. XXI, *de ref.,* c. 4.

[35] ". . . Sed et hoc necessarium instituere duximus, ut plures ecclesiae uni nequaquam committantur presbytero, quia solus per totas ecclesias nec offitium valet persolvere nec rebus earum necessariam curam impendere, ea scilicet ratione praecipimus, ut ecclesia, que usque ad decem habuerit mancipia super se habeat sacerdotem, que vero minus aliis coniugatur ecclesiis."—C. 3, C. X, qu. 3.

[36] Can. 3—Harduin, III, 1796.

[37] Cf. Leage, R. W., *Roman Private Law* (London, MacMillan, 1932), p. 96, for classical meaning.

[38] Fagnanus, *Commentarium* in lib. III, tit. 48, c. 3, n. 28.

[39] Corradus, *Praxis Beneficiaria,* Lib. III, cap. 5, n. 10; S. R. Rota, *Florent.,* May 22, 1630, decis. 380, n. 8 and 29, part. 5, *recent.* tom. II, p. 739.

Leurenius, following Corradus, maintains that at least ten families are needed, and he too bases his opinion on the wording of Gratian and on the Rota decision.[40]

The most reasonable explanation is the one which can be reconciled with the glossator of Gratian and the apparently incompatible decision of the Rota, and which supports the common opinion. Probably all were concerned with ten persons, not in the sense of indiscriminate human beings, but in designation of persons with legal personality and capacity, namely the *patresfamilias*. These as the heads of distinct families were the ones who were counted along with all those who were comprised in their families. In Germany parishes were erected in some places where there were less than ten Catholic families, but where there were enough Protestant families to raise the total to ten or more.[41] Doctrinally this viewpoint is of course defensible. Since heretics and schismatics are subjects of the Church and obtain no exemption on account of their heresy or schism, they too are subject to the pastor of their place of residence. But canonically the ruling seems to deal with actual, rather than merely prospective, Catholic families. No modern canonist holds that a population of less than ten Catholic families suffices for the establishment of a new parish.

[40] Leurenius, *Forum Beneficiale*, Pars. I, q. 160. See also Barbosa,—*Jus Ecclesiasticum Universum*, Lib. I, cap. 20, n. 16;—*De Officio et Potestate Parochi*, I, 1, n. 20; De Luca, *De Parochis*, disc. 23, n. 17; Pirhing, *Jus Canonicum*, lib. III, tit. 29, n. 1.

[41] Schmalzgrueber, *Jus Ecclesiasticum*, III, tit. 29, n. 7; Rossi, *De Paroecia*, p. 21.

CHAPTER V.

THE PROCEDURE IN DETAIL

Canon 1428. § 1.—Locorum Ordinarii uniones, translationes, divisiones, dismembrationes beneficiorum ne faciant nisi per authenticam scripturam, auditis Capitulo cathedrali et iis, si qui sint, quorum intersit, praesertim rectoribus ecclesiarum.

Art. 1. *Consultation.*

When the ordinary thinks that a new parish is needed, before he proceeds with the actual founding he is bound to obtain moral certainty that the necessary canonical cause is present and to decide whether the erection is justified under the circumstances. He is left free to ascertain the facts in any manner he thinks best, by a sort of canonical non-judicial process.[1] Usually he will make a local inspection either personally or through a delegate. The rural dean could well be selected as his delegate.[2] The importance of determining the actual existence of the cause lies in the fact that division made without a cause is invalid.[3] Even with a cause the new foundation may be faced with almost insuperable obstacles to its successful operation. Furthermore, the prudent bishop will not depend for facts on biased testimony of interested parties, lest he be later embarrassed by being asked to defend his course of action after someone has had recourse to the Holy See.[4]

But more is required than even such a conscientious investigation. The ordinary is obliged to hear the cathedral chapter (or

[1] Wernz, *Jus Decretalium,* II, n. 267; S. R. Rota, *Lucana,* Apr. 13, 1917—AAS, IX (1917), 512.

[2] Leurenius, *Forum Beneficiale,* pars. I, q. 157, n. 2.

[3] Can. 1428, § 2.

[4] The bishop of Sion, in Switzerland, was commended by the Rota for having made a summary investigation, by sending a dean as his delegate to ascertain the facts before he proceeded to divide the parish,—*Decisiones,* IV (1912), 157, n. 7; AAS, IV (1912), 457.

diocesan consultors in places where they substitute for the cathedral chapter) and any persons who may be interested, especially the rectors of the churches.[5] In the missions the prefect or vicar apostolic should obtain the counsel of his consultors according to the prescriptions of can. 302 and 303.[6]

Although the legal practice under the old law gave some reason for doubt,[7] the common opinion was that the cathedral chapter must not only be heard, but that their consent was most probably required under the pain of nullity.[8] The reason was because on the one hand division of a parish involved the alienation of some of the assets of one benefice in order to make the new one possible,[9] and on the other hand the consent of the chapter was always required for valid alienation.[10] Furthermore, since the consent was explicitly demanded in the law for the valid union of parishes, it was argued that consent was necessary in the same way for division.[11]

Shortly before 1918 the question was raised whether an erection

[5] Can. 1428, § 1.

[6] S. C. Prop. Fid., *Instructio,* Jul. 25, 1920, n. 2—AAS, XII (1920), 331.

[7] ASS, III (1867), 396, appendix VI.

[8] The Rota held that there was no value to the opposite opinion: "Inter has solemnitates consensus capituli certe requiritur ad substantiam seu sub poena nullitatis, nisi forte v. g., in divisione paroeciarum etiam exemptorum regularium, episcopus procedit tamquam delegatus Sedis apostolicae vel (uti gr. in Gallia) consuetudine aliud obtineat." *Sedunen.,* Apr. 2, 1912—*Decisiones,* IV (1912), 154, n. 5.

[9] Abbas Panorm., *Lectura* in lib. III Decret., tit. 48, c. 3, n. 2; S. C. C., *Dismembrationis,* Sept. 16, 1871—ASS, VII (1872), 41; De Luca, *De Decimis,* disc. 12, n. 8; S. R. Rota, *Sedunen.,* Apr. 2, 1912, *loc. cit.*

[10] C. 1, X, *de his quae fiunt a praelato sine consensu capituli,* III, 10; Reiffenstuel, *Jus Canonicum Universum,* lib. III, tit. 48, n. 19. The Council of Trent made one exception to this general rule by allowing the bishop to act "tamquam Sedis Apostolicae delegatus" when dividing exempt parishes. As delegate he did not need such consent for validity. See Schmalzgrueber, *Jus Ecclesiasticum,* III, tit. 48, n. 20 and 21.

[11] The Rota argued: "Omnis res per quascumque causas nascitur per easdem dissolvitur." *Sedunen.,* Apr. 2, 1912—*Decisiones,* IV (1912), 154, n. 5; c. 2, *de rebus ecclesiae non alienandis,* III, 4, in Clem.

of a parish was invalid by reason of the fact that the consent given by the cathedral chapter was for a more restricted procedure than that which the bishop decreed. In answer to the question the auditors of the Rota pointed out that the consent of the chapter was required substantially under pain of invalidity, but not specifically for the manner and form in which the division was to be made.[12]

The Code makes special mention of the rectors of the churches among those whose interests are involved. The consent of the pastor is not required in the present law, nor was it necessary under the Decretal or Tridentine Law. In the Constitution of Alexander III nothing is to be found referring to the consent of the pastor; on the contrary, it is decreed that the pastor cannot hinder the undertaking.[13] Tridentine and present law both include the phrase *"etiam invitis rectoribus,"* thereby meaning of course unreasonable unwillingness. Pastors are reasonably unwilling, and hence deserve to be heeded, if there is serious doubt about the existence of a canonical cause. The reason why the consent of pastors is not required is because the salvation of the souls of parishioners is in question, and private interests must yield to the public good. What is said of pastors applies equally to patrons.

But, although at no time, past or present, has the consent of the pastor or that of the people been necessary in the division of a parish, the question arose whether the bishop was bound to summon and consult the pastor for advice before preceeding to the division, and whether, if the citation was neglected, the act was null or rescissible. The older opinion under the old law held that the citation and hearing were necessary for validity. While it was not necessary that the objections or suggestions of the pastor influence the decision of the bishop in any way, still the law presumed that because of his proximity to the people and his first hand knowledge of local conditions the priest could be expected to be an exceptionally well qualified, though perhaps biased, witness to the existence or lack of existence of the essential

[12] S. R. Rota, *Sedunen.*, Apr. 2, 1912, *loc. cit.*

[13] C. 3, X, *de ecclesiis aedificandis vel reparandis,* III, 48.

canonical cause. To omit to cite and hear the rector of the parish within the confines of which another parish was to be established was to neglect an essential formality which the law provided as a defense against unnecessary alienation of property.[14]

To deny a hearing to the pastor was unjustly to deny him the opportunity belonging to him in law to prove, if in the particular instance proof was possible, that the alleged reason for division could be adequately eliminated by the assignment of curates. Of course, if the pastor could prove that point, then there was no canonically valid cause for division.[15] During the half century preceding the Code the contrary opinion came into favor, by which canonists more commonly taught that the consultation with the pastor, rather than constituting an essential form of the process, was only a solemnity pertaining to licitness and intended to promote a better understanding of the facts in each case, and to prevent hasty, ill-advised action.[16]

The Code now groups together in one phrase the consultors and all other interested parties, especially the rectors of the churches. The same law, therefore, applies to all of them in the same manner.

The Code substantially derogates the old law in the matter of the consent to be obtained from consultors. According to canon 1428, § 1, now it is not necessary for the ordinary to obtain the consent of the cathedral chapter, or of the consultors where they supply for the chapter according to can. 427, but only their opinions. This canon clearly forbids the bishop to divide a parish without first getting the advice of his consultors. The advice must not be obtained from the consultors singly, but while they are gathered together at one time, and they are obligated to give their

[14] S. C. C. *Nullius,* Sept. 22, 1600—*Fontes,* n. 2335; Corradus, *Praxis Beneficiaria,* lib. III, c. 2, n. 4; *Fagnanus, Commentarium* in lib. III, tit. 48, c. 3, n. 29; Pirhing, *Jus Canonicum,* lib. III, tit. 48, n. 11.

[15] Reiffenstuel, *Jus Canonicum Universum,* lib. III, tit. 48, n. 15.

[16] ASS, III (1867), 400, appendix VI. See also S. R. Rota, *Londonen.,* Aug. 21, 1914—AAS, VII (1915), 75; S. R. Rota, *Sedunen.,* Apr. 2, 1912, n. 5—*Decisiones,* IV (1912), 154. Cf. also Rucupis, "The Canonical Formation of Parishes and Missions," *Amer. Eccles. Review,* LV (1916), 245; Wernz, *Ius Decretalium,* II, n. 267.

opinions honestly. It would not be prudent to disregard an opinion which has the support of several councilors, and the legislator urges ordinaries not to go against it without proportionately grave reasons.[17]

The Code continues the old law as it was more commonly interpreted as regards the consultation of all other interested parties. Regarding the citation and hearing of those whose interests are involved, a distinction is to be made between those who have rights in connection with the administration of the old parish, such as the pastor and the patron, and others who have no title to any such rights, but who nevertheless may incur inconveniences from the division, namely, the parishioners. This distinction is of importance only because the legislator shows special eagerness to grant a hearing to those most vitally interested. The opinion of the parishioners may frequently be of real value to the bishop, particularly where considerable financial problems are at stake, where a trustee system is in force, or where there is danger that action may give rise to discord and recourse; oftentimes astute business men may be equipped to give especially valuable advice as to the most advantageous time and place for a proposed division. Nevertheless, in no sense is the consent of the people necessary for valid action. In fact, prior to the Code, once a decision had been made canonically, even despite the vigorous opposition of the people, they could still be compelled to support the new church.[18]

It is not necessary to hear the parishioners individually. A good plan would be to announce a public meeting, inviting all interested parties to attend. They could discuss the proposed change and choose one or more delegates to represent them before the bishop. Another plan would be to consult the trustees in places where the trustee system exists.

Still another factor that deserves special consideration is the possibility that certain persons may in equity deserve a special hearing. Granting that a parishioner or a benefactor, for example,

[17] Can. 105, 1°.

[18] Conc. Trident., sess. XXI, *de ref.*, c. 4. See S. R. Rota, *Sedunen.*, Apr. 2, 1912—*Decisiones*, IV (1912), 153, n. 5.

who has made more than his share of contributions to the building fund of the older parish does not thereby obtain any right in justice to be heard when division is being considered, nevertheless a spirit of fair play should enter into such transactions. Perhaps the presence of the new parochial church in a certain neighborhood may do serious financial harm to the owner of valuable business property in the vicinity. Equity would be better served if such persons as these were to be given an opportunity to state their cases individually.

Where the parish is vacant, it is not possible to cite and hear the pastor in the normal way. In such a case a special *parish defender* might be appointed by the bishop to take the place of the pastor at the consultation.[19]

There remains the question whether the obligation to cite the consultors or other interested parties, particularly the rectors of the churches, and to ask their advice obliges under pain of nullity, or whether the neglect of this obligation would nevertheless leave the act of division valid and legally recognized.

If taken by itself, canon 1428, § 1, does not make any reference to nullity. Furthermore, according to canon 11 and canon 1680, § 1, only those acts are null which are expressly or equivalently declared null by the law. If these three canons are considered alone the conclusion is that the hearing is not required for validity. Nullity of any act is odious and should not be presumed, but must be clearly proven. It is noteworthy than canon 1416 which prescribes that before the erection of a benefice interested parties must be cited and heard, is without a nullifying clause. The more common opinion holds than canon 105, 1°, settles the question, because it uses the exact phrase of canon 1428—*audito capitulo*—as

[19] Although this prescription of the old law is not renewed in the Code, the retention of the practice would be an excellent safeguard for equity. This was never specified directly in the law, but it was gathered indirectly from c. 2, *de rebus ecclesiae non alienandis*, III, c. 4., in Clem., where it was decreed that a union of benefices made without citing the rector or defender is nevertheless valid.

an example of a nullifying clause.[20] But against that opinion there is a serious objection. Several authors believe than canon 105, 1°, probably is not at all concerned with the validity or invalidity which would result upon overlooking the formality of hearing the parties referred to, but solely with the secondary purpose of contrasting the effects of advice and consent. Canon 105, 1°, apparently only contrasts the effects of consent and advice *after* the specific canons elsewhere in the Code equivalently or expressly state the nullifying effect of omitting the formality. Canon 105, 1°, states that the hearing is enough for validity: it does not follow that what is enough is necessarily required.[21] If that opinion is correct, and it does seem tenable, canon 105, 1°, has no bearing on the problem under discussion.

While the arguments of those maintaining the invalidating effects of this part of canon 105, 1°, are in harmony with the more obvious—and seemingly more correct—meaning of the text, nevertheless in the face of the solid opinion to the contrary the best solution would be to apply canons 11 and 15 and declare the consultation necessary for lawfulness, but not for validity. The authentic solution to the problem long since proposed to the Commission for interpretation[22] is still awaited. Bastnagel, after a thorough comparative study of the authors who take sides in the controversy, concludes that persons concerned should not be disturbed about the validity of acts performed in violation of the second clause of canon 105, 1°.[23]

[20] Rossi, *De Paroecia*, p. 30; Coronata, *Institutiones*, I, n. 153, footnote 8; Vermeersch-Creusen, *Epitome*, I, n. 229, footnote.

[21] See Vermeersch-Creusen, *loc cit.*, for a lengthy discussion of this somewhat plausible opinion. Cicognani (*Canon Law*, p. 506) approves the opinion of Vermeersch.

[22] See Vermeersch-Creusen, *Epitome*, I, n. 197 bis; Coronata, *Institutiones*, I, n. 153, footnote 8.

[23] *The Appointment of Parochial Adjutants and Assistants*, p. 206-228, especially p. 228. Among others who agree with him are Vermeersch-Creusen, *Epitome*, II, n. 758; Ayrinhac, *Administrative Legislation*, p. 328. Among those who defend the necessity of this consultation for validity are Coronata, *Institutiones*, II, n. 983, p. 377, footnote 8; De Meester, *Compen-*

Art. 2. *Boundaries*

Another formality in the erection of a parish is the assignment of a territory with boundaries which must be fixed clearly, permanently, and immutably.[24] There are no serious difficulties springing from the law itself, nor were there any under the old law. The cases decided by the Roman tribunals and congregations involving parish boundaries were practically all concerned, not with the law itself, but with the reconstruction of facts where documentary evidence was missing. One looks in vain for an elaborate treatment of the legal aspect of boundary questions because the law is, and has been, too obvious to be mistaken.[25]

Parochial limits are permanent, because to interfere with them involves the division or dismemberment of a benefice, which can only be accomplished when there is a canonical cause. It is to be noted that boundaries are not identified with the marker by which they are designated. Consequently they should not be designated by transitory objects, such as buildings, or by city limits without more particular specification, especially if there is danger that such entities can become a source of confusion by being shifted or expanded by civil authorities.[26] Any shifting of the marker does not affect the actual parish limit, although it might destroy the possibility of determining the boundary precisely. Permanent natural landmarks such as rivers, hills, and lakes generally offer safe markers from which to determine boundaries. City streets and federal, state, or county highways, especially when they run on section lines, or political boundaries, as well as railroad right-of-ways would also serve this purpose adequately.

National parishes, or any others of a nature primarily personal, are specified rather by the people who belong to them than by

dium, n. 1410, p. 388; Rossi, *De Paroecia,* p. 30; Augustine, *Canonical and Civil Status,* p. 168, footnote 53.

[24] S. R. Rota, *Bononien.,* Jul. 21, 1911—*Decisiones,* III (1911), 357, n. 6.

[25] Conc. Trid., sess. XXIV, *de ref.,* c. 13; can. 216, § 1.

[26] S. R. Rota, *Annecien.,* Feb. 5, 1918; *Derthon.,* Jan. 31, 1919—AAS, XI (1919), 151; 473.

their territorial limits. Often such parishes have territorial boundaries as a secondary principle of division.

In drawing parish boundaries the prescriptions of canon law regarding canonical causes for division should be the principal directive norm. The purpose of the division is to eliminate great difficulty of approach for a notable portion of the population (at least ten families), and to lessen congestion in an overcrowded parish. Once that purpose has been taken care of, there is a further norm. Although the necessity of the people is the only justification for making the division in the first place, the convenience of the people plays a leading rôle in determining the balance of territory and population between the new and the old parishes. As long as a sufficient population remains to support the pastor and to maintain the physical equipment of the old parish there is no reason why the new parish may not contain within its borders territory that is not difficult of approach to the church in the old parish; nor is there any reason why some of the families that could be accommodated easily by the old parish should not be assigned to the new one. The new parish may need the extra families for its decent support. The laity will usually attend, if not the nearest, at least the most convenient church, and their convenience should be taken into consideration. Either reason would justify the ordinary in setting the boundary closer to the older church than is necessary strictly to satisfy the demands of the canonical causes.

The boundaries of quasi-parishes in mission countries subject to the Congregation for the Propagation of the Faith should be clearly set forth in the decree of erection. If it is not possible to set exact territorial boundaries, the ordinary should at least designate which Christian communities belong to each.[27]

[27] "Erectio quasi-paroeciae fiat per decretum Ordinarii, quo clare describantur territorii limites. Ubi vero practice hoc obtineri non possit, sufficit declarasse quae christianitates ad singulas quasi-paroecias pertineant. Decreto insuper statuatur quae sit ecclesia principalis quasi-paroeciae, nec non residentia quasi-parochi." S. C. Prop. Fid., *Instructio,* Jul. 25, 1920, n. 4—AAS, XII (1920), 331. The same sacred Congregation extended the rule

Art. 3. *Decree of Erection*

Canon 216, § 1, lists the elements that suffice for the constitution of parishes but is silent about the act by which parishes are founded. It simply says: "let dioceses be divided." Whenever all the elements therein prescribed concur the law recognizes the group as a parish.

Since no canonical moral person can exist which does not derive its authority from the Church[28] no parish can begin to exist as a moral unit except by the authority of the Church. Canon 100, § 1, denotes the two ways in which moral personality can be conferred: either by a prescription of the law itself or else by the special concession of a competent ecclesiastical superior given by means of a formal decree.

The second of these ways is the one by which a parish is erected, namely, by the formal decree of a competent superior. True, nowhere does the Code explicitly demand a formal decree for the erection of a parish, but canon 1418 orders that the establishment of benefices be accomplished by means of a document, and canon 1428, § 1, forbids local ordinaries to unite, transfer, divide, or dismember benefices except by an authentic writ. Parishes are benefices[29]. The Sacred Consistorial Congregation declared in regard to former mission dioceses that to constitute parishes a decree of the ordinary is required.[30] A similar regulation for the missions was contained in an instruction of the S. Congregation for the Propagation of the Faith.[31]

It is therefore certain beyond all doubt that the only lawful way of founding a new parish is by means of a formal decree of the local ordinary, *i.e.*, a decree which determines accurately all the elements to be comprised in the new foundation. The law

here laid down for quasi-parishes to parishes in mission dioceses. *Decree,* Dec. 9, 1920—AAS, XIII (1921), 17.

[28] Brown, *The Canonical Juristic Personality,* pp. 91-92.

[29] See chapt. IV, art. I, of this work.

[31] S. C. Prop. Fid., instr. Jul. 25, 1920, nn. 4, 5—AAS, XII (1920), 331.

[30] S. C. Consist., declar. Aug. 1, 1919, n. 2—AAS, XI (1919), 346.

insists also that it be in writing, although, strictly speaking, as the S. Congregation of the Council observed, the authentic writ or document is not the same thing as the formal decree of erection.[32]

Neither the old nor the new law demand the formal decree of erection as a condition for a valid foundation. The S. Congregation of the Council held that the canonical constitution did not depend entirely upon the formal decree but that it resulted also from the realization of the other elements which go to make up a parish, namely, a definite territory bound by definite limits, a community of the faithful, a rector or pastor exercising the care of souls, and finally the authority of the bishop maintaining and approving this juristic condition.[33]

The old discipline continues up to the present time, despite the opinion of one author to the contrary.[34] The reasons for maintaining that the law has not been changed are these: first, the new law makes no mention of invalidity resulting from failure to issue a formal decree. Since nullity is legally odious and must never be presumed in any case where the law is even doubtful[35] there is no reason for believing that the requirement is for validity here.

Secondly, according to the reply of Cardinal Gasparri, Chairman of the Pontifical Commission, to the Apostolic Delegate to the United States, Sept. 26, 1921, a special decree of the ordinary is not necessary for the erection of a parish but it is sufficient that the ordinary define the territorial limits and assign a rector to the people and the church within said limits.[36]

Finally, the S. Congregation of the Council based its decision on the same legal grounds in solving a difficulty presented by the bishop of Prince Albert and Saskatoon regarding the obligation of

[32] S. C. C., *Principis Alberten. et Saskatoonen., Missa pro populo,* Mar. 5, 1932—AAS, XXV (1933), 436-438.

[33] S. C. C., litt. Mar. 18, 1881—*Collectanea,* II, n. 1548.

[34] Pistocchi. *De Re Beneficiali,* p. 130.

[35] Can. 11.

[36] Bouscaren, *Canon Law Digest,* I, 149.

priests to say the *missa pro populo* in parishes which had never been formally decreed. In the discussion of the law involved it was pointed out by the Congregation that, while no formal decree had ever been issued, nevertheless by actually attributing to the parish the titles, rights and obligations that customarily belong exclusively to parishes and pastors the bishop had given approval that amounted to an implicit or tacit decree.[37]

In practice the document and formal decree mean the same thing, although strictly speaking they are not identical, as has already been observed above. In reality the decree is the act of the bishop; the document is the proof of the act. The purposes of the document are to set forth accurately all the facts pertinent to the erection of the new benefice and to forestall uncertainty in the future. The document should describe the boundaries, the site of the parish church, the endowment, if any, and the other sources of income which are expected to be sufficient for the maintenance of divine worship and for the support of the clergy, and finally the declaration whether the status of the pastor is to be removable or irremovable.[38]

The document did not receive any attention from the lawmakers until the latter part of the past century. The law of the Decretals and of the Council of Trent make no mention of it. It is, however, by no means a new invention, because authors offered several formulae, but without abundant commentary.[39]

It might be noted here that the hierarchical unit of which the parish is part determines the status of the parish. The ultimate perfect territorial subdivisions of a diocese are parishes; those of a vicariate or prefecture apostolic are quasi-parishes. When a vicariate or prefecture becomes a diocese, its quasi-parishes automatically become parishes without the need of any formal decree.[40]

[37] S. C. C., *Principis Alberten. et Saskatoonen.*, Mar. 5, 1932—AAS, XXV (1933), 436-438. Cf. Maroto's commentary on this response in *Apollinaris*, VI (1933), 423-431.

[38] S. C. Consist., declar. Aug. 1, 1919,—AAS, XI (1919), 346.

[39] Corradus, *Praxis Beneficiaria*, lib. III, cap. 2, n. 11; Bouix, *De Parocho*, appendix I, p. 671.

[40] Can. 216, § 3.

The law for the missions orders that two copies of the decree should be made, one to be preserved in the archives of the diocese or prefecture or vicariate apostolic, the other in the files of the parish or quasi-parish.[41] That would be an excellent rule to follow in fully organized dioceses.

For sample document see Appendix.

Art. 4. *Means of Support*

Canon 1427, § 3.—Paroeciam dividens, Ordinarius debet vicariae perpetuae aut paroeciae noviter erectae congruam portionem assignare, servato praescripto can. 1500; quae, nisi aliunde haberi queat, desumi debet ex reditibus ad ecclesiam matricem quoquo modo pertinentibus, dummodo sufficientes reditus eidem matrici ecclesiae remaneant.

Canon 1415, § 3.—Non prohibetur tamen, ubi congrua dos constitui nequeat, paroecias aut quasi-paroecias erigere, si prudenter praevideat ea quae necessaria sunt aliunde non defutura.

The source of material support for a parish gives rise to many considerations.

First, regarding a parish that comes into being by means of creation according to canon 216, § 1, the Code has nothing to say about a source of income. But no argument can be drawn from that silence, because other considerations remove all doubt that an income is necessary.

Secondly, regarding a parish that comes into existence by means of division from a previous parochial territory, canon 1427, § 2, orders that the ordinary should assign to the new parish or permanent vicarage a fitting share of property *(congrua portio)*.

Thirdly, the source of the income is to be an endowment consisting of a share of the goods belonging to the mother church, if an

[41] S. C. Prop. Fid., Jul. 25, and Dec. 1, 1920—AAS, XII (1920), 331, and XIII (1921), 17.

endowment cannot be obtained by some other kind of reliable payments, and provided the resources of the mother parish permit. Or, in case of necessity, any kind of support will do, provided it be reliable.

In the ancient law, according to which the bishop was the sole administrator of all the goods of every church in the diocese, the offerings of the faithful belonged to the common fund from which was taken what was necessary for the expenses of worship, for the poor, and for the livelihood of the sacred ministers.[42] When the parishes began to be taken care of by permanent vicars with actual responsibility for the spiritual and temporal administration, the necessity arose to provide them with the livelihood which they could no longer expect from the table of the bishop. Before the middle of the VI century precautions were taken against the danger of a church failing to fulfil its purpose because of a dearth of material resources. The laity were encouraged to build and endow churches, and they in return were granted certain privileges regarding the appointment of the clergy who were attached to these churches.[43] The Emperor Justinian, about 540, prescribed that before establishing a new church the founder should consult the bishop and state what funds he is willing to provide for the necessities of divine worship, for the upkeep of the building, and for the support of those who care for the church and for charity to the poor. The general custom of endowing churches came to be looked upon as the one principal source of support. Particular statutes forbade the dedication of a church until it had an endowment sufficient to care for all of the ordinary expenses of the church. So long did these laws remain in force that they eventually found their way into the decree of Gratian.[44]

[42] Const. of Pope Gelasius—c. 23, C. XII, q. 2.

[43] Godfrey, *The Right of Patronage according to the Code of Canon Law*, p. 64.

[44] "Nemo ecclesiam edificet ante, quam civitatis episcopus veniat, et ibidem crucem figat, publice atrium designet, et ante prefiniat, qui edificare vult, que ad luminaria, et ad custodiam, et stipendia custodum sufficiant, et ostensa donatione sic domum edificet, et post, quam consecrata fuerit, atrium eiusdem ecclesiae sancta aqua conspergat."—C. 9, Dist. I, *de cons.* The Decree

Pope Innocent III at the IV Lateran Council condemned the practice that existed in some places by which patrons, who retained the administration of church goods, left to the priests serving the altar a portion so small that they could not be decently supported. He complained that as a result the clergy were not given to study, and he ordered that the vicar in charge of a parish should receive a decent livelihood *(congrua portio)*.[45] Bishops were even forbidden to ordain clerics without providing them the necessities of life, not merely the bare necessities required for food and lodging, but in addition enough to meet other moderate current and extraordinary expenses.[46]

The Council of Trent was solicitous that the needs of both the rector and the parish be provided in keeping with their dignity.[47]

AMOUNT OF SUPPORT REQUIRED

Because the purpose of these laws has not changed, the Church has not abrogated or derogated any of them by lessening the financial requirements except in the matter of specific kinds of payments, including tithes and first fruits. The parochial patrimony

assigns the authorship of this canon to a council of Orleans, but Berardi *(Gratiani Canones Genuini ab Apocryphis Discreti,* pars I, cap. 29) says that it can be found only in the *Novels,* LXVIII, 2. See also III Council of Braga (572), c. 5—Mansi, IX, 839; Kremer, *Church Support in the United States,* p. 15; Leurenius, *Forum Beneficiale,* pars I, q. 22.

[45] C. 30, X, *de praebendis et dignitatibus,* III, 5; IV Lateran Council (1215), c. 32—Schroeder, *Disciplinary Decrees of General Councils,* p. 269 and 573.

[46] C. 2, 10, 12, X, *de praebendis et dignitatibus,* III, 5; c. 2, *de decimis, primitiis et oblationibus,* III, 13, in VI°; Schmalzgrueber, *Jus Ecclesiasticum,* lib. III, tit. 48, n. 22; S. R. Rota, *Bobien.,* Mar. 4, 1911, n. 12—*Decisiones,* III, (1911), 111.

[47] "In parochialibus etiam ecclesiis quarum fructus adeo exigui sunt ut debitis nequeant oneribus satisfacere, curabit Episcopus, si per beneficiorum unionem, non tamen regularium, id fieri non possit, ut primitiarum vel decimarum assignatione, aut per parochianorum symbola ad collectas, aut qua commodiori ei videbitur ratione, tantum redigatur quod pro rectoris ac parochiae necessitate decenter sufficiat . . ."—Conc. Trid., sess. XXIV, *de ref.,* c. 13.

which is stipulated in canon 1427, § 3, is the sum total of all the temporal goods, whether they be tangible or intangible, movable or immovable, which belong to the parish as a moral person. It includes endowment, funds or future income of any nature that accrue to the parish for parochial purposes. Because the parish and the benefice are distinct moral persons so also is the property of each distinct. For that reason the parochial patrimony of canon 1427, § 3, is specifically distinct from the beneficial endowment of canon 1410.

As Bernier accurately points out, the parochial patrimony is composed of two classes of goods: those belonging to the parish as a whole, and those belonging to the parochial church as a church—a distinction that is of practical importance especially where parishes have been erected in churches that do not belong to the parish, for example in cathedral churches, or churches belonging to religious institutes. Of course in this latter instance the goods of the church are not part of the parish patrimony. Otherwise, as is commonly the case, the church itself belongs to the parish, and consequently the property belonging to the church is parish property.[48]

The parish patrimony must in most instances suffice to erect and maintain the permanent equipment, such as the church building, which is one of the elements necessary for a parish,[49] and the parochial residence.[50] The entire cost of the building program need

[48] P. Bernier: "De Patrimonio Paroeciali," *Jus Pontificium*, XVII (1937), 235-241.

[49] Can. 216, § 1; 1162, § 2. An exception would apply if the church is not exclusively parish property and has an independent source of support.

[50] A parish house, while it is to be supplied if possible, is not absolutely required. The rule under the old law was that, if the parish could not bear the cost of building a residence for the clergy, a house might be rented within the bounds of the parish or, if none could be rented within the parish, the pastor could live beyond but near its boundaries. S. C. C., *Reatina*, Jun. 3, 1592—*Fontes*, n. 2245. The Code places upon pastors the obligation of residing near their church: "Parochus obligatione tenetur residendi in domo paroeciali prope suam ecclesiam; loci tamen Ordinarius potest iusta de causa permittere ut alibi commoretur, dummodo domus ab ecclesia paroeciali non ita distet ut paroecialium perfunctio munerum aliquid inde detrimenti capiat"—can. 465, § 1.

not be defrayed immediately, if it is prudently foreseen that the income will be large enough to retire the debt within reasonable time. A debt too heavy to be retired in a reasonable time is equivalent to an insufficient endowment.

Ancient legislation regarding the income sufficient to maintain sacred worship remains in force. Under this heading fall occasional expenses for repairs to the equipment and replacements of worn vestments and vessels, the cost of providing materials used at divine services, as well as any other costs that can reasonably be expected to occur.

Since the income is established for the sake of maintaining a moral person, which is of its nature permanent, it follows that whatever be the source of the income, it too must be "certain and perpetual, and not subject to any danger of loss."[51] It has, of course, been impossible to set any definite figure by general law, on account of the fluctuations in the value of money and the difference in the cost and standard of living at different places and times. Attempts have been made to set a sum permanently for particular localities, but the figures decided upon have had to be interpreted soon afterward relatively to the circumstances affecting the purchasing power of money and the needs of the place.[52]

Canon 1410[53] indicates what sources are suitable to supply the endowment that is a requisite condition for the establishing of a benefice. It has long been a practice in places where invested funds or fruitful property cannot be obtained to follow canon

[51] Can. 1415, § 1; S. C. C., *Quebecen.*, Jul. 14, 1917—AAS, X (1918), 196; S. C. C., *Fanen., Erectionis,* Mar. 22, 1760—*Thes. Resol.*, XXIV (1760), 57.

[52] Pius V, const. *"Ad exsequendum,"* Nov. 1, 1567—*Bullarium Taurinen.*, VI, 228; S. C. C., *Tudertina*, Apr. 27, 1822—Pallottini, *Collectio Conclusionum S. C. C.*, XIV, 542, n. 90; Conc. Trident., sess. XXIV, *de ref.*, c. 13.

[53] Can. 1410: "Dotem beneficii constituunt sive bona quorum proprietas est penes ipsum ens iuridicum, sive certae et debitae praestationes alicuius familiae vel personae moralis, sive certae et voluntariae fidelium oblationes, quae ad beneficii rectorem spectent, sive iura, ut dicitur, stolae intra fines taxationis dioecesanae vel legitimae consuetudinis, sive chorales distributiones, exclusa tertia earundem parte, si omnes reditus beneficii choralibus distributionibus constent."

1410 (which is directly concerned with benefices) as a norm for supplying a patrimony for the parish moral person.[54] Therefore, among the graduated sources with which the bishop may choose to compose the parish patrimony are the following: goods owned by the moral person (endowment in a strict sense), or definite payments due by some family or moral person, or voluntary but reliable contributions of the faithful which accrue to the rector, or stole fees within the limits set by diocesan statute or lawful custom.[55] If these are not available or if, when taken individually or collectively, they prove to be insufficient, the bishop may make up the necessary balance by deducting it from the funds of the mother church, provided sufficient income remains for the support of the old parish.[56] Finally, if none of these sources is adequately available, the bishop is not forbidden to erect a new parish without an endowment, if he is morally certain that the needed support will not be lacking anyhow.[57]

What has thus far been said of the amount required for the patrimony of a parish presupposes the establishment of a distinct beneficial endowment as defined in canon 1410. In cases where, because of the absence of a separate endowment, the pastor and his assistants are to receive their support from the common funds of the parish it is evident that the parish must receive a patrimony adequate to support the parish clergy in a condition sufficiently respectable that they need not become odious to the people by being forced to exact rigidly the emoluments which are normally uncertain.[58] The Church expects her sacred ministers to "live by the altar" in such a manner that they do not need to perform non-clerical work to the neglect of the care of souls, and that they need not undertake unbecoming tasks that might lessen the respect of the people for the priesthood.[59]

[54] Pistocchi *(De Re Beneficiali,* p. 122-123), thinks the parallel application of canon 1410 with canon 1427, § 3, is entirely justified.

[55] According to the parallel provisions of can. 1410.

[56] Can. 1427, § 3.

[57] Can. 1415, § 3.

[58] S. C. C., *Potentina,* Mai. 19, 1906—*Thes. Resol.,* CLXV (1906), 581.

[59] Pallottini, *Collectio Conclusionum S. C. C.,* XIV, p. 536, n. 66.

ENDOWMENT AS A MEANS OF SUPPORT

The endowment method, strictly considered, is that by which one or more persons assign to the ownership of the moral person, as a trust fund for the expenses of building and for the upkeep of divine worship, goods of any kind, preferably immovables, although any kind of goods, even bonds, will suffice, provided the income be certain and perpetual.[60] It is the most satisfactory method for both Church and people, because it leaves the least uncertainty for the future financial security of the parish by providing a certain and permanent income. So helpful was the endowment system to the Church that, to encourage it, she developed the system of patronage, by which laics who built and endowed churches were granted certain privileges in connection with the appointment of the clergy who were attached thereto.[61] The Church still places the stamp of approval upon the establishment of endowments. But because experience has shown her that patronage is often an obstacle to the good administration of dioceses, she wishes to abolish or restrict the institute of patronage as far as this is compatible with already acquired rights. Although she no longer grants the right of patronage, she nevertheless permits the ordinary to grant other spiritual favors, temporary or perpetual, proportioned to the liberality of the grant; for instance, an annual mass. He may also permit the founder to designate the first pastor.[62] He may allow the founder, in the act of founding the endowment of the new parish, to place conditions even contrary to the common law, provided they are not unbecoming and not repugnant to the nature of the parish.[63] Another sign of the favor in which endowments are held by the Church is her decreased reluctance in allowing new foundations whenever the proper endowment is offered.[64]

[60] Leurenius, *Forum Beneficiale,* par. 1, q. 8; Wernz, *Ius Decretalium,* III, n. 182.

[61] Godfrey, *Right of Patronage in the Code,* p. 39-41.

[62] Can. 1450, §§ 1 and 2. Kremer, *Church Support in U. S.*, p. 69.

[63] Can. 1417, § 1.

[64] S. R. Rota, *Sedunen.*, Apr. 2, 1912—*Decisiones,* IV (1912), 158, n. 9; S. R. Rota, *Bobien.*, Mar. 4, 1911, n. 12—*Decisiones,* III (1911), 110, n. 12.

The goods owned by the moral person are of their very nature an endowment whenever they are annexed to the parish for the sake of its support. When the endowment consists of a sum of money the ordinary, after consulting his board of administration organized according to the rules of canon 1520, should invest the money in safe and fruitful real estate or bonds.[65]

State aid has one of the important advantages of an endowment in that it gives an assurance of continuous support. On the other had, it has given rise to much harmful interference by the civil authorities in purely ecclesiastical affairs.[66] Where state aid is arranged by concordat it is acceptable as a supplementary or sole endowment.[67]

RELIABLE CONTRIBUTIONS OF THE FAITHFUL

The certain contributions of the faithful are considered equivalent to an endowment. Consequently, in a broad sense the Church accepts as a form of endowment certain goods to which the moral person will receive the title only in the future. The suitable revenue is considered provided if, instead of receiving property, such as land or real estate or money, the parish is sure of income from such sources as payments due by some family or moral person, from voluntary but reliable contributions of the faithful which accrue to the rector for parochial purposes, or from stole fees within the limits set by diocesan regulation or lawful custom. All of these payments and fees are not necessarily endowment, but may be made such by a declaration of the bishop.[68]

It is to be noted that payments from a family or moral person must be due to the parish by some title of justice, in order to guarantee the permanency of the payments. A mortgage on the property of the family or moral person, or perpetual obligations imposed on a family or community by testament would provide

[65] Can. 1415, § 2. See Wernz, *Ius Decretalium*, III, n. 153.

[66] Kremer, *Church Support in the U. S.*, p. 55-56.

[67] Vermeersch-Creusen, *Epitome*, II, n. 743.

[68] Can. 1410.

such a guarantee.[69] The contributions of the faithful, on the contrary, need not be due in justice, but they must be reliable. They may take any of several forms. The time-honored system of tithes[70] designates the contribution to religion of the tenth part of all produce and profits derived either from annual crops (predial tithes) or from personal industry (personal tithes). By the sixth century it was widely prescribed in church law,[71] and from the eighth to the tenth century it was enforced by civil law. After a period when tithes had been accurately regulated by universal Church law,[72] custom gradually forced the system into desuetude in many places, until it has become quite exceptional in modern times. The equally ancient system of contributing the first fruits for the support of the Church has become even more universally obsolete than the tithe system.[73] The Code leaves existing conditions unchanged, prescribing that local statutes and customs are to be observed as far as the payment of tithes and first fruits is concerned.[74] Parishes can still be found which depend on tithes for their support.[75]

The prospective offerings of the faithful are considered to be a suitable patrimony, provided the payments themselves are substantially reliable, that is, provided it is certain that payments will be made, even though the amount is indefinite.[76] Customary col-

[69] Pistocchi, *De Re Beneficiali*, p. 20; Vermeersch-Creusen, *Epitome*, II, n. 743; Leurenius, *Forum Beneficiale*, pars I, q. 8.

[70] *Deuteronomy*, XIV, 22; *Leviticus*, XXVII.

[71] Doheny, *Church Property: Modes of Acquisition*, p. 46.

[72] Cc. 1-35, X, *de decimis, primitiis et oblationibus*, III, 30.

[73] *Exodus*, XXIII, 16; Barbosa, *Iuris Ecclesiastici Universi Libri Tres*, III, 25, 7.

[74] Can. 1502. Cf. Kremer, *Church Support in the U. S.*, p. 43.

[75] S. C. Consist., *Resol., Tarvisina, et Patavina*, Jul. 16, 1932—AAS, XXV (1933), 470-472. In the United States the system has been introduced in Des Moines, Iowa, and in Elkhart, Indiana, with good results. In 1927 the Catholics of the Diocese of Seattle were asked to give four per cent of their income for church support. See Kremer, *op. cit.*, p. 37.

[76] S. C. C., *Sabinen.*, Jun. 27, 1807—*Thes. Resol.*, LXXIII (1807), 130; Vermeersch-Creusen, *Epitome*, II, n. 743.

lections or subscriptions of free-will offerings made for the support of the parish at certain regular intervals usually yield a sufficiently stable annual income. Pew rent and offertory collections, which form the main support of the Church in the United States, are also to be classed as dependable voluntary offerings that qualify as a source of endowment for a parish. The reason why free-will offerings are reliable enough to be considered perpetually safe is to be found in the moral obligation of Catholics to contribute whatever is necessary for the support of their church. Although under the present law no sanction is attached to the non-fulfilment of the duty, nevertheless Catholics do not look upon regular contributions as purely spontaneous and gratuitous offerings, but rather as the fulfilment of a moral obligation.[77] Formerly the faithful could be compelled to contribute to the support of the pastor of the new parish.[78]

In times prior to the Code it was disputed whether stole fees could ever be considered part of the endowment of a benefice.[79] It is now clear that they can be employed for this end,[80] and it appears, as a consequence that they may be assigned to the parish patrimony. The common law grants *stole fees* to the pastor as his personal property, because primarily they have the nature of a remuneration from individuals for special services rendered on particular occasions, and are not inherently characterized as the fulfilment of an obligation arising from his benefice, or his position as administrator of parish property. In like manner, the levies or fees receivable for the various acts of voluntary jurisdiction, or for the execution of rescripts, or for the administration of the sacraments and sacramentals belong to the pastor personally. He has a right to demand them only if the amount of the fees has been approved by the Holy See according to the rule of canon

[77] For a detailed treatment of the obligation of Church support, see Kremer, *Church Support in the United States*, p. 38-54.

[78] Conc. Trident., sess. XXI, *de ref.*, c. 4.

[79] Wernz, *Ius Decretalium*, III, n. 183. For negative opinion see S. C. C., *Sabinen.*, Jun. 27, 1807—*Thes. Resol.*, LXXIII (1807), 130.

[80] Can. 1410; S. C. C., *Quebecen.*, Jul. 14, 1917—AAS, X (1918), 198.

1507, § 1.[81] In view of this right granted to pastors by the common law, the exception granted in canon 1410, by which levies and stole fees may be made part of the endowment, must not be presumed unless there are no other revenues, but must be precisely determined in a decree of the local ordinary at the time when the parish is erected.[82] An ordinary will not avail himself of his power to take away a privilege granted by the common law, unless he has a correspondingly good reason, namely, one of commonly acknowledged necessity.

When stole fees are included by the ordinary in the endowment of the benefice or of the parish, only the amount "within the limits of diocesan assessment or legitimate custom need be surrendered by the pastor, even when the faithful spontaneously make more generous offerings."[83]

Mass stipends cannot be included in the endowment if they are manual masses, because they are in no wise connected with the benefice, but are purely personal obligations. Vermeersch seems to put foundation masses in the same class with stole fees.[84]

COMMON PROPERTY OF CANON 1500 SOMETIMES A MEANS OF SUPPORT

After prescribing the assignment of a suitable income to a newly erected parish, canon 1427, § 3, calls attention to canon 1500, which should not be overlooked.

> **Canon 1500.—Diviso territorio personae moralis ecclesiasticae ita ut vel illius pars alii personae morali uniatur, vel distincta persona moralis pro parte dismembrata erigatur, etiam bona communia quae in commodum totius territorii erant destinata, et aes alienum quod pro toto territorio contractum fuerat, ab auctoritate ecclesiastica, cui divisio competat, cum debita propor-**

[81] Can. 463, § 1.

[82] S. C. C., *Canarien.*, Jul. 16, 1927—AAS, XX (1928), 391, n. 3.

[83] Ferry, *Stole Fees*, p. 61.

[84] *Epitome*, II, n. 743. He follows Wernz, *Ius Decretalium*, III, n. 183.

tione ex bono et aequo dividi debent, salvis piorum fundatorum seu oblatorum voluntatibus, iuribus legitime quaesitis, ac legibus peculiaribus, quibus persona moralis regatur.

The common property which is the subject of canon 1500 should not be confused with the parochial patrimony because the two are specifically distinct, although actually they may sometimes serve the same purpose. Consequently, common property is treated here as a possible source of suitable support.

When a parish is erected into a moral person it is thereby made capable of enjoying rights, such as the right to possess property, and is made capable of bearing burdens, such as debts. By its erection it can be said to be incorporated. This means that its scope, its duties, and its rights are defined and are in a sense organically connected with it. The parish corporation has the right of ownership or permanent usufruct over its patrimony which is either decided upon and assigned to it by the bishop, or is otherwise legitimately acquired by the parish. This parochial property is something which cannot be separated from the parish corporation without alienating a right that belongs to the parish as a moral person.

On the contrary, the common property with which canon 1500 deals may or may not be incorporated with the moral person, according as the title to it is or is not vested in the parish. It is not the fruit of the endowment of the parish, even the surplus fruit, but it is that which arises from an extrinsic source, for instance, from special collections or donations. It has not been acquired absolutely by the common treasury of the parish but remains earmarked for some common good of the territory as a whole. Common property embraces funds or assets of any kind intended for any pious or charitable purpose. The purpose might be the care of the sick or the poor, or the education of children, or the social betterment of all the inhabitants of the district. The funds might be the sum gathered by means of special collections for extra-parochial purposes, such as diocesan assessments, Peter's Pence, or other similar charities. If, before the division, collections and donations had been gathered throughout the extent of the old parish for a building fund for a new church, such a fund would likewise be common property intended for the welfare of the whole territory, and should be equitably divided.

Goods designated for a particular local purpose are not affected by the division, because the legislator insists that the wishes of pious founders or donors, the legitimately acquired rights and the local laws prevail over these prescriptions of the general law.[85]

What has been said of common goods applies equally to liabilities incurred for the sake of a purpose common to the whole territory. If the benefit for which the debt was incurred continues to apply to the new parish, as well as to the old, the debt is to be divided. A school, for example or a hospital that continues to serve both parishes should not be the burden of only one of them. But, if the school or hospital is intended to serve only one parish, then it is no longer a common liability.

Canon 1500 prescribes that the common goods be divided justly and equitably between the new and the old parishes. The canon expresses an obligation, not solely a permission. Common funds retain their former purpose after the division, and are to be applied accordingly, without being restricted to the diminished territory of the old parish.[86] The equitable division of common property and debts should be done by the ecclesiastical authority which makes the division of the parishes. It appears from this that property and debts do not, by a mere operation of the law, pass to the moral person in whose annexed territory the property is vested or the debts are contracted, but both of these are to be apportioned by an act of the bishop.[87]

The division is not to be made arbitrarily, but insofar as it may

[85] Ayrinhac, *Administrative Legislation*, p. 38.

[86] See Augustine, *Canonical and Civil Status of Catholic Parishes*, pp. 171-174; also his *Commentary*, VI, 558; Ayrinhac, *Administrative Legislation*, p. 387; De Meester, *Juris Canonici Compendium*, vol. III, pars I, 336; Pistocchi, *De Re Beneficiali*, p. 120.

[87] S. C. C., *Resolutio, Tarvisina et Patavina*, Jul. 16, 1932—AAS, XXV (1933), 470-472.

be possible and feasible, it should be made in proportion to the balance of territory and population of the two parishes. Because it is impossible to strike a mathematical balance between all factors, the bishop, after taking into account the relative importance and conditions of the divided territory, is to make the allotment in the way that he considers most just and most fair to all parties. The nature of the partition of the common property and debts is administrative. Consultation of those who are interested is not prescribed, as long as these cannot lay claim to any of the particular vested rights mentioned in canon 1500.[88]

ENDOWMENT FROM REVENUE OF MOTHER CHURCH

If necessary, the mother church may be assessed to make up the endowment necessary for the support of the filial church, but not if it is otherwise possible to obtain suitable independent support for the new territory by means of a new extrinsic endowment or probably from any of the other steady sources of income listed in canon 1410, or from the common property of canon 1500 which has not been destined by the donor for some other purpose. There has been no fundamental departure from the former discipline.[89] No type of property belonging to the mother church is exempt from the levy. Consequently, any of the property, payments, offerings or even stole fees within the qualifications indicated in canon 1410, as well as revenues from unspecified donations and bequests or from any other source are assessable.[90]

The bishop, however, must carefully provide that the material resources of older churches shall not be put in jeopardy when new

[88] Pistocchi, *De Re Beneficiali*, p. 120; Ayrinhac, *Administrative Legislation*, p. 338.

[89] "Illis autem sacerdotibus, qui de novo erunt ecclesiis noviter erectis praeficiendi, competens assignetur portio, arbitrio episcopi, ex fructibus ad ecclesiam matricem quomodocumque pertinentibus."—Conc. Trident., sess. XXI, *de ref.*, c. 4. See Bouix, *De Parocho*, p. 273.

[90] Pistocchi, *De Re Beneficiali*, p. 122; Augustine, *Canonical and Civil Status of Parishes*, p. 175.

ones are created. Therefore, the mother church must not be assessed so heavily that a sufficient income no longer remains for its own maintenance. The law does not of itself give to the filial parish any right over the goods of the mother parish. It merely authorizes and orders the bishop, whenever it be necessary, to take part of these goods as an endowment for the filial church, if that can be accomplished without serious harm to the mother church.[91]

The authorization given to alienate part of the property of a mother church for the support of its filial church is to be interpreted strictly, because alienation of the goods of a benefice is a legally odious matter. The relationship between mother church and filial church is sometimes incorrectly spoken of when that existing between major and minor churches is actually meant, for example, when the churches in a given locality are of greater or less dignity by reason of antiquity or in view of special privileges. The use of the terms "mother" and "filial" to signify the relationship of a parish church to a succursal chapel, whose chaplain cares for the people of a certain section of the parish, is also incorrect, because the chapel with its territory has not been erected into a moral person, but remains part of the large parish, whereas the filial church must be entirely independent in the exercise of the care of souls. The relationship to which canon 1427, § 3, refers is one of origin. It arises when one or more new parishes or permanent vicarages are formed from the people and the territory of the original parish.[92] The assessment for the filial church cannot be laid on the mother church after the decree of erection has already been issued, because the filial church must be *newly* erected to qualify for relief. In fact, the parish which is erected by division from the territory of another is not filial at all unless it receives at least part of its endowment from the original parish.[93] No

[91] C. 44, C. XVI, q. 1; *Capit. ad Salz.*, (803), c. 3—MGH, *Leges*, I, ed. Pertz, 124; S. C. C., *Bergomen.*, Aug. 22, 1908—*Thes. Resol.*, CLXVIII (1908), 651.

[92] S. C. C., *Caietana*, Aug. 10, 1917—AAS, X (1918), 460; De Luca, *De Decimis*, disc. 12, nn. 12-13.

[93] Pistocchi, *De Re Beneficiali*, p. 14, footnote; S. C. C., *Aversana, Matricitatis*, Jun. 13, 1931—AAS, XXV (1933), 208-211.

permission is granted to assess the goods of a parish for the support of any other which is not filial to it by origin, nor was this permission granted under the old law.[94]

> **Canon 1427, §4.—Si vicaria perpetua aut nova paroecia dotetur ex reditibus ecclesiae a qua dividitur, debet matrici honorem deferre modo et finibus ab Ordinario praestituendis: qui tamen vetatur baptismalem fontem matrici ipsi reservare.**

The filial church should pay honor to the mother church which endows it. The local ordinary in the decree of erection should determine precisely the manner and extent of the marks of honor. Under the old law of the Decretals the right of patronage over the new parish belonged to the rector of the mother church whenever the revenues of the latter supplied the endowment of the new church.[95] Formerly it was permitted to reserve to the mother church certain signs of recognition implying the retention of traces of her former jurisdiction in the old territory, which were signs to be tendered by the filial church in view of its derived territory and assured revenues of endowment from the mother church. Marks of that kind included the right of conducting all burials, of receiving tithes, or receiving from the filial church an annual tribute.[96] Other signs that were permitted were the reservation to the pastor of the mother church of the right of performing solemn functions on certain days of the year, for example, on the patronal feast day, the obligation of the pastor of the filial church to assist at liturgical functions in the mother church on certain more solemn feast days of the year, and the reservation of the baptismal font to the mother church.[97] Any of the foregoing tradi-

[94] Fagnanus, *Commentarium,* lib. III, tit. 48, c. 3, n. 32.

[95] ". . . et in ea (ecclesia nova) sacerdotem . . . ad praesentationem rectoris ecclesiae maioris cum canonico fundatoris assensu instituas . . . "—c. 3, X, *de ecclesiis aedificandis vel reparandis,* III, 48. See Bouix, *De Parocho,* p. 277.

[96] S. C. C., *Aversana, Matricitatis,* Jun. 13, 1931—AAS, XXV (1933), 208 ff; Schmalzgrueber, *Jus Ecclesiasticum,* lib. III, tit. 48, n. 19.

[97] Cappello, *Periodica,* XXII (1933), 160.

tional signs of deference would seem to be acceptable nowadays, except those which are forbidden by law. Thus, the present law no longer allows the bishop to reserve the baptismal font to the mother church, but every parochial church must have its own baptismal font, "any statute, privilege, or custom to the contrary notwithstanding."[98] Nor is the right of patronage to be granted to the rector of any church which in the future endows its filial church.[99] Because the Code does not explicitly exclude any other of the traditional signs of honor, it would seem that any of them can still be ordered by the bishop . An appropriate commemorative tablet conspicuously located at the filial church would be an effective way of paying the honor due to the original church.

SUPPORT WITHOUT ENDOWMENT

Canon 1415, §3.—Non prohibetur tamen, ubi congrua dos constitui nequeat, paroecias aut quasi-paroecias erigere, si prudenter praevideat ea quae necessaria sunt aliunde non defutura.

Finally, since the Code became effective, the local ordinary is not forbidden to erect parishes or quasi-parishes where any adequate endowment cannot be provided, if he has moral certainty that the necessities for support will never be lacking. This canon is a concession made for the good of souls, but the reluctance of the legislator is apparent from the negative wording of the text. Even where the canonical causes are present, together with the minimum financial security demanded by this canon, the bishop is not under obligation to proceed to the erection of a new parish. He is simply granted permission to do so if he thinks that the circumstances justify it.

In so far as moral certainty is required regarding an income sufficient perpetually to maintain the parish and its ministers, § 3 of canon 1415 does not differ at all from § 1 of the same canon,

[98] Can. 774, § 1.

[99] Can. 1450, § 1.

which prescribes that a suitable endowment must be perpetual. It does, however, differ notably in this, that it does not require that the source of income be permanently and specifically determined at the time when the new parish is founded. The bishop must have some kind of guarantee that income from some source will always be adequate. Thus, even when he could assign at best a partially sufficient endowment to the parish, he might foresee that the diocese will always have a missionary fund to supply the deficit in poor localities. Another alternative would be to unite with the parochial benefice another benefice of the type that does not involve the care of souls or the obligation of residence, and which therefore is not incompatible with the pastorate, e.g., a mass foundation erected by the bishop. This could be done in accordance with the prescriptions of canons 1419, 3°, 1420, § 3, and 1423, § 1.[1] The final decision as to whether the necessary support is sufficiently well guaranteed rests with the bishop.

If he cannot have moral certainty that even this last source of income will not fall below what is a necessary minimum, the bishop may not do more than designate subsidiary churches or chaplaincies within the boundaries of some parish upon which they shall remain dependent for a time until enough revenues are available to support them independently.[2]

There had been considerable uncertainty in the United States, even after the publication of the Code, as to the status of territorial subdivisions existing within dioceses and having all the other qualities of true parishes, but lacking the endowment element of canon 1410. The Apostolic Delegate, on Nov. 10, 1922, conveyed to the bishops of the United States a reply from Cardinal Gasparri, Chairman of the Pontifical Commission for Interpretation, regarding the necessity of a formal decree for the valid erection of parishes. After answering the questions that had been submitted, the Cardinal asserted that a parish is always an ecclesiastical benefice according to canon 1411, 5°, whether it has the proper

[1] This was taken for granted by the Council of Trent (sess. XXIV, *de ref.*, c. 13).

[2] S. C. Consist., declar. Aug. 1, 1919—AAS, XI (1919), 346.

endowment (resources or revenue) as described in canon 1410 or even if lacking such an endowment (resources or revenue) it be erected according to the provisions of canon 1415, § 3.[3]

The opinion is ventured that there is still room for discussion whether some of the parishes in the United States can be considered genuine benefices as defined in canon 1409, because the means of support seem to belong to the parish as such rather than to the distinct parochial benefice. The Apostolic Delegate had this distinction in mind when he framed the questions for the Commission, for he asked: "whether for the erection of a parish which has not the nature of a benefice . . . etc." Cardinal Gasparri in his reply may have been referring only to the practice in certain American dioceses whereby the offerings of the faithful at Christmas and Easter accrue to the pastor personally as the fruits of his benefice. Possibly also, he did not wish to discuss what seems to be a quite common practice in the United States, of constituting a parish patrimony along the lines indicated by canons 1410 and 1415, §3, without establishing a distinct beneficial endowment. According to the letter of the law only the first practice (i.e., of granting annual collections to the pastor) would provide the endowment which is essential to a benefice.

This distinction must not be overstressed, however, because canons 1410 and 1415, § 3, appear to have been framed to meet conditions similar to those in the United States. It is not unlikely that the legislator with this in mind wished to consider as benefices even those parishes which do not have a separate source of revenue for the beneficial endowment, but where, nevertheless, adequate provision is made for the support of the clergy from the parish funds. Pastors in this country generally receive their support and a moderate salary from the common treasury of the parish. In view of canon 1410, perhaps this salary can be constituted a benefice by the bishop because it consists of "reliable payments due from a moral person."

[3] Bouscaren, *Canon Law Digest,* I, 149.

Art. 5. *Assignment of a Pastor and a Parish Church.*

THE PASTOR

Canon 454, § 3.—Novae (paroeciae) quae erigantur, sint inamovibiles, nisi Episcopus, prudenti suo arbitrio, attentis peculiaribus locorum ac personarum adiunctis, audito Capitulo, amovibilitatem magis expedire decreverit.

§ 4.—Quasi-paroeciae sunt omnes amovibiles.

Canon 216, § 1, lists among the factors that constitute a parish or quasi-parish the assignment of a particular rector, who as its special pastor is to exercise the care of souls therein. Because the canon is not, strictly speaking a definition, it must be interpreted in the light of other canons.

As has been discussed in a previous chapter, a parish is a benefice. From this it is clear that one of its component parts is the sacred office, which in this case is the care of souls. But it is also a moral person, and therefore perpetual, i.e., it can exist even when there is no priest incumbent in the sacred office. The fact that the parish can be vacant at all proves that the decree of erection produces only the sacred office, not the parish priest. On the other hand the office would be meaningless if in its normal state it were not filled. Without a pastor it is deprived of its fully proper function, and its vacancy reveals an abnormal state. The bishop is ordinarily obliged to see that the office is not vacant longer than six months.[4] Since the scope of this dissertation is limited to matters that bear directly upon the canonical erection of parishes, there is no place here for a lengthy discussion of the questions relating to the qualifications of the priest or moral person who holds the office of pastor, or to the manner of making the appointment.

The stability of the incumbent in office depends upon the choice of the bishop at the time of the founding of the parish. All pastors should be appointed for life. This general rule is not affected by

[4] Can. 458.

the dual possibility that they may have been appointed either as removable or as irremovable pastors.[5] Nevertheless the permanency of their appointment is not absolute, for in the presence of a sufficient canonical cause any pastor may be removed whenever the salvation of souls or the welfare of the Church is unmistakably jeopardized by his continuation in the pastoral office. When the occasion requires it, he may be validly removed by one of two processes. The shorter process is sufficient in the case of removable pastors;[6] a lengthier one is required for irremovable pastors.[7] The stability of the pastor in office is not a personal privilege belonging to the man; it is a status conferred by the type of benefice which he holds. Newly erected parishes by law call for the appointment of irremovable pastors unless the bishop, upon prudent inspection of the particular local and personal circumstances and upon consultation with the cathedral chapter (or body of diocesan consultors) decrees that it is more expedient to employ the appointment of removable pastors. If the bishop decides to put the new pastoral incumbent and his successors in the class of removable pastors, he must include this decision in the decree which attests the new erection of the parish. Even if he decides to let the preference of the law rule in the case by making the new pastor irremovable, he should, for reasons of prudence, certify this intention at the time when the canonical erection of the parish takes place. His decision should also be included in the written document of foundation in order to prevent all uncertainty in the future.

This question cannot arise in regard to quasi-parishes, because by law their pastoral incumbents are all removable. A special rule applies to dioceses subject to the S. Congregation for the Propagation of the Faith. Although the subdivisions of these dioceses are known as parishes, they are subject to the regulations for quasi-parishes; hence their pastors are by law removable.[8]

Religious pastors are removable without any specified canonical

[5] Can. 1438.

[6] Can. 2157-2161.

[7] Can. 2147-2156.

[8] S. C. Prop. Fid., decr. Dec. 9, 1920—AAS, XIII (1921), 17.

process. But in their case also, as in all cases of appointment to ecclesiastical incumbencies, it is the presence of some equitable cause, and not the arbitrary will of authority, that furnishes a basis for their removal from office.[9]

THE PARISH CHURCH

Every parish should have a parish church.[10] There is a case on record in which two parishes were officially permitted to share a common parish church temporarily.[11] But when the Sacred Congregation of the Council made this concession, it did so "although it is much more fitting that to each parish a particular church be assigned as soon as possible.[12]

Another case of relevant import was submitted to the same Congregation for a decision. It concerned the offering of the *missa pro populo* by three pastors whose congregations used the same church for their parochial services. It was argued that although it was quite incongrous that distinct parishes should not have their own churches, nevertheless the common participation in the use of one and the same parochial church did not prevent the separate existence of three distinct parishes. The Sacred Congregation approved of the line of argument advanced by the consultor, for it forbade the three pastors to take their turn in the celebration of a single *missa pro populo* on the required days and ordered each of them personally to fulfil the obligation of this mass on all the days when such obligation existed.[13]

The Code has nothing to say about the building of parish churches in particular, so that the regulations governing the construction of churches in general must be applied. Regulations governing the construction and blessing and equipment of a church are to be found in canons 1161-1169.

[9] Can. 454, § 5.

[10] Can. 216, § 1.

[11] S. C. C., *Feltrien.*, Jul. 15, 1882—ASS, XV (1882), 309-325.

[12] *Ibidem*, p. 324.

[13] S. C. C., *Consentina*, Jun. 12, 1917 and Feb. 9, 1918—AAS, X (1918), 285-289.

There should also be a parish house for the pastor near his church. The bishop may, for a just reason, allow the pastor to live elsewhere provided the place is not so distant from the parochial church that the performance of pastoral duties is impaired.[14] An instruction of the S. Congregation of the Propaganda for mission countries directs the bishop to designate the principal church of each parish or quasi-parish and also the residence of the quasi-pastor.[15]

Art. 6. *Recourse*

Canon 1428, § 3.—Adversus decretum Ordinarii . . . dividentis beneficia, datur in devolutivo tantum recursus ad Sanctam Sedem.

Against the decree of the ordinary who divides a benefice recourse may be had to the Holy See. Such recourse, however, does not suspend the operation of the decree. Formerly, in the case of a division of parishes exempt from the ordinary power of the bishop because united *pleno iure* to a religious institute this recourse was to be made directly to the Holy See, because the bishop acted as a delegate of the Holy See when he proceeded to divide such parishes. In the case of other parishes it could be made either directly to the Holy See or also to the metropolitan.[16] The Decretals forbade all appeal (recourse) against the division of a parish,[17] but practically all the authors interpreted the prohibition as forbidding that kind of recourse which would suspend the operation of the decree. There were no authors who insisted that no redress could be sought with the possible hope that the decree might be nullified by the Holy See.[18]

To protect her own interests and those of all concerned, the Church offers a remedy against an injudicious decree of the bishop.

14 Can. 465, § 1.

15 July 25, 1920—AAS, XII (1920), 331, n. 4.

16 Cf. Bouix, *De Parocho*, p. 282.

17 ". . . sublato appellationis obstaculo, . . . appellationis cessante diffugio." —c. 3, X, *de ecclesiis aedificandis vel reparandis*, III, 48.

18 Cf. Bouix, *De Parocho*, p. 280.

Although the ordinary is given wide discretionary powers to decide whether the facts in each specific case are in harmony with the rules prescribed by the legislator, he is given no license to deviate from these rules, even when they cannot be observed without great inconvenience. The ordinary is the one who decides whether a canonical cause is present, or whether the endowment is sufficient, and how the details of the division are to be arranged.

Under the present law the recourse is to be taken directly to the Holy See. The metropolitan is no longer competent. Canon 1601 says: "Against the decrees of ordinaries appeal or recourse is not permitted to be taken to the Sacred Rota; but the Sacred Congregations exclusively handle recourses of that kind." The competent authority within the Holy See is the Sacred Congregation of the Council, which has jurisdiction in matters affecting benefices.[19] If the recourse is made from mission territory the S. Congregation of the Propaganda is competent.[20] The reason why the recourse is not made to the Rota is this: since the act of the bishop in dividing a parish is administrative, and not judicial, it is brought to a conclusion by the issuance of a decree, and not by the passing of a sentence. Appeal from a sentence is taken to a court of higher instance; recourse from an administrative decree is taken to a superior administrator. That is the normal procedure. In exceptional cases, namely, when the one having recourse has positive reason to believe that he still has not received a just decision from the S. Congregation of the Council, he may appeal directly to the Holy Father, who will leave it to Apostolic Signatura to decide whether the case should be tried by the Rota according to canon 1603, § 2. Before the constitution *"Sapienti consilio"* of June 29, 1908, jurisdiction was not so clearly defined.

The occasion for taking recourse is not limited by law. The decree may be attacked on any grounds. It may be attacked as invalid because of the lack of some essential condition. It may be attacked as rescissible, because it is thought to be impracticable. or as working too great hardship on a part of the community, or

19 Can. 250, § 2.
20 Can. 252, § 3.

as injuring the rights and privileges of any interested person or group of persons without sufficient cause.

The effect of recourse is *in devolutivo*, i.e., even while the recourse is pending the decree of the ordinary is effective. The presumption is that the bishop acted reasonably. The burden of proof in doubtful cases rests upon the one entering the recourse. As a precaution against being asked to defend himself against charges of overhasty and ill-considered action in erecting parishes, the bishop will find it to his advantage to preserve the reports rendered by his advisors before the division.[21]

The petitioner should send to the S. Congregation the document issued by the bishop, and he should briefly and accurately state the reasons why he believes the act of the bishop to be invalid or unjustified in the circumstances. Augustine points out that it would be well for the petitioner to give a reference to former decisions in similar cases.[22]

As to the time within which recourse must be taken the canon is silent. In certain other cases the Code permits recourse only within ten days, e.g., in canons 1465, § 1; 1709, § 3; and 2153, § 1, but since it places no such restriction on recourse against the decree of the bishop in dividing a parish it appears that according to the letter of the law as it stands the recourse may be taken at any time. On the other hand a parallel case has arisen which gives an indication of what the ruling of the Holy See will probably be if a delayed petition for recourse against the division of a parish is ever presented. Canon 2146, § 1, is silent about the time within which recourse is to be taken against certain specified decrees of the ordinary, including the removal of pastors. Yet, regarding this canon 2146, § 1, the S. Congregation of the Council specifies a limit of ten days.[23] There is a certain parity between canon 2146, § 1, and canon 1428, § 3, in this regard. The difference is merely one of effect in the recourse itself, in as far

[21] For an example of a well defended case see S. R. Rota, *Sedunen.*, Apr. 2, 1912—*Decisiones*, IV (1912), 149; AAS, IV (1912), 457.

[22] *Canonical and Civil Status of Catholic Parishes*, p. 180.

[23] S. C. C., resol. Jan. 14, 1924—AAS, XVI (1024), 162-165.

as the recourse, according to canon 2146, § 3, suspends the effect of the bishop's act only partially. Surely it would not be in harmony with equity to permit anyone to put off making his recourse until the building units of the newly constituted parish are already under construction.

CHAPTER VI

RELIGIOUS AND NATIONAL PARISHES

Art. 1. *Establishment of Religious Parishes*

Canon 452, § 1.—Sine Apostolicae Sedis indulto paroecia nequit personae morali pleno iure uniri, ita nempe ut ipsamet persona moralis sit parochus, ad normam can. 1423, § 2.

§ 2.—Persona moralis, cui paroecia sit pleno iure unita, habitualem tantum curam animarum retinere potest, servato, quod ad actualem spectat, praescripto can. 471.

Canon 1423, § 2.—Nequeunt vero (Ordinarii) paroeciam unire . . . cum monasteriis, ecclesiis religiosorum.

Essentially the characters of secular and religious parishes are identical. It is therefore imperative to distinguish between the establishment of a parish and its union with some particular religious institute, because of itself the parish remains the same moral person regardless of whether it be conferred on a secular priest or whether it be united with a religious institute. In point of time the founding of a parish and its incorporation with some religious institute are not all necessarily identical. The original constitution of the parish may long precede its later union with any specific religious institute.

The term "religious parish" is often used in a broad sense to signify any kind of connection between a parish and a religious institute. There are four distinct ways by which this connection may be realized. The first is the most complete possible union (*plenissimo iure*), and is said to exist when episcopal or quasi-episcopal jurisdiction over the clergy and the people of the incorporated parish is transferred from the diocesan local ordinary to the abbot of the monastery to which the parish is united. This kind of incorporation is to be found in the union of parishes with territorially independent abbacies.[1]

On the other hand there is union with full right (*pleno iure*) when the parish is united to the religious institute in such a way that the institute is the permanent (*habitualis*) pastor and the actual pastor, who is always a religious, is nominated by the superior and approved and appointed by the bishop. The parish is not exempted entirely from the power of the local ordinary but remains subject to his jurisdiction, visitation, and coercive power, in matters pertaining to the care of souls.[2] It is noteworthy that the Code reserves the phrase "religious parish" to this type.[3]

A third kind of union (*ad temporalia tantum,* or *semi-pleno iure*) occurs when the religious house participates only in the fruits of the parochial endowment and has charge of the administration of the temporalities, while the actual pastor must be a secular priest. A parish of this kind is secular, not religious.[4]

Finally, parishes may sometimes be committed to the care of religious without being united in any way to the institute. The parish remains secular although it is actually administered both in spiritual and temporal affairs by the religious pastor.

Because the normal means of administering the care of souls in a diocese is by means of the secular clergy working under the bishop, the Code prescribes that all new parishes are by law secular even when their foundation results from the partition of a religious parish.[5]

The union *plenissimo iure* is by its nature reserved to the Holy See by canon 215, § 1.

The union *pleno iure* cannot be accomplished by the bishop,

[1] Wernz-Vidal, *Ius Canonicum,* II, n. 154.

[2] Can. 452; 456; 1425, § 2; 471, § 1.

[3] Can. 1425, § 2.

[4] Can. 1425, § 1.

[5] Can. 1427, § 5. This is a continuation of the old law as upheld by S. C. C., *Brixinen.,* Feb. 16, Mar. 16, 1743—*Fontes,* n. 3548.

because canon 452, § 1 (cited at the head of this article), declares that the local ordinary is incapable of doing so without an indult of the Holy See. There is no doubt that a union attempted in violation of this canon would be invalid because the wording of the canon leaves no room for any other interpretation.

Even the union *non pleno iure* which unites a parish with a religious house as to temporalities only *(semi-pleno iure),* i.e., in such a way that the religious house acquires the right to the revenues of the parish but not to its spiritual administration, is likewise reserved to the Holy See.[6]

There still remains the problem of parishes entrusted to the care of religious without being in any way united to the community. The Code explicitly forbids the conferring of secular benefices on religious.[7] Furthermore, the conferring of secular benefices not permanently but for a time only is likewise forbidden by the general law.[8] Consequently, for the bishop on his own authority to confer secular benefices temporarily on religious is against the common law. However, the S. Congregation for the Propagation of the Faith has granted special faculties to bishops in mission countries to appoint members of the regular clergy to parishes whenever suitable priests are not available.[9] Outside of the missions, in countries subject to the whole common law of the church the Apostolic Delegate is empowered "to grant to local ordinaries in particular cases or for a time the faculty of placing religious in charge of parishes when secular priests are not available, but always with the consent of the religious superiors, and with the understanding that at least two other religious shall live with the pastor, and observing in other respects the dispositions of the sacred canons."[10]

From what has been said it follows that only by indult can

[6] Can. 1423, § 2 and 1425, § 1.

[7] Can. 1442.

[8] Can. 1438.

[9] S. C. Prop. Fid., decr. Dec. 9, 1920, n. 3—AAS, XIII (1921), 17.

[10] Bouscaren, *Canon Law Digest,* I, 184.

a parish be united to a religious institute; otherwise, when a parish is entrusted to religious in virtue of special faculties but without an indult the institute as such does not acquire any pastoral rights, and the parish does not become religious, but remains secular.

When there are reasons why it is desirable to unite a parish with a religious community application may be made to the Holy See for an indult granting permission for the contemplated union.

The application for the indult should be made by means of two documents; one drawn up by the ordinary and the other by the religious community. Each document should contain the reasons for the desired union, and an accurate description of the boundaries of the parish. The bishop should also state that he has complied with the other prescriptions of the Code that apply in this case. He should not omit to mention that he has heard the consultors and others who are interested. If any special agreements between the ordinary and the community have been made, they should be clearly and accurately set forth in the documents. The document of the bishop should be sent to the S. Congregation of the Council, and that of the religious institute to the S. Congregation of Religious. Both documents should be headed: "Beatissime Pater," even though they are sent directly to the Roman curia and not to the Holy Father personally.[11]

With the exception of the national, lingual, personal, and familial parishes which, according to canon 216, § 4, are subject to change only by indult of the Holy See, the bishop is competent to divide any and all other parishes, including those which are fully incorporated with an exempt religious institute, provided only that there be present such reasons as canonically justify the

[11] Through the procurator of the religious: see can. 517. The S. Consistorial Congregation decided that the faculty of granting secular parishes to religious belongs to the S. Congregation of the Council, but there remains the obligation for religious orders and congregations of obtaining from the S. Congregation of Religious the necessary faculty or dispensation, if their constitutions and rules forbid them to hold or administer parishes: S. C. Consist., July 5, 1915-AAS, VII (1915), 327. Cf. also Coronata, *Institutiones,* I, n. 469; *Augustine, Canonical and Civil Status,* p. 80.

making of a division. In the absence of any apostolic indult to the contrary the newly erected parish will always be classified as a secular parish. It enjoys this status regardless of the type of parish from which it was cut off. The reservation to the Holy See by canon 1422 of every division or dismemberment of a religious benefice is indeed a general law. As such this law would also comprise the reservation of *parochial* religious benefices, if its scope and application remained without restriction or qualification. But the ruling of canon 1427, § 1,—that ordinaries are capable of dividing all parishes whatsoever *(paroecias quaslibet)*—prevails as a particular exception to this general law on religious benefices. Canon 1427, § 1, in reference to canon 1422 simply illustrates and verifies the principle that "generi per speciem derogatur." The opinion of Rossi that canon 1422, by reason of being more particular, prevails over canon 1427, §1, is not held by other canonists, nor does Rossi give any reasons for his view.[12] The power of the diocesan ordinary to divide religious parishes and his consequent obligation of assigning the newly erected parishes to the diocesan clergy are points which both were contained in the old law.[13] The difference between past and present law rests in the fact that formerly the power was delegated whilst now it is ordinary.[14]

While maintaining the right of the local ordinary to divide the parishes of exempt religious, Augustine adds a pertinent suggestion: "However, since an incorporated parish of religious can only be obtained by the Holy See (can. 452; can. 1425), it would seem rather presumptuous for an Ordinary to proceed to a division or

[12] *De Paroecia*, p. 24.

[13] Leo XIII, const. *"Romanos Pontifices,"* Mai. 8, 1881, nn. 15 and 16—*Fontes*, n. 582. The Pope declares that this constitution, although specifically adapted to settle disputes and difficulties peculiar to England to whose hierarchy it was addressed in general is but a restatement of the common law (nn. 4 and 5), Consequently the legal principles contained therein are universally binding. Because similar conditions had developed in the United States the particular directive norms of the constitution were extended also to this country in 1885.

[14] See chapt. IV, art. 1, of this work.

dismemberment without informing the Apostolic See. This seems at least a reasonable assumption, especially since the boundaries of every religious parish are accepted and sanctioned by the Holy See."[15] Because the Code nowhere prescribes such a notification it is not required either for the validity or for the lawfulness of the procedure.

Art. 2. *Establishment of National or Language Parishes*

Canon 216, § 4.—Non possunt sine speciali apostolico indulto constitui paroeciae pro diversitate sermonis seu nationis fidelium in eadem civitate vel territorio degentium, nec paroeciae mere familiares aut personales; ad constitutas autem quod attinet, nihil innovandum, inconsulta Apostolica Sede.

The Church has recognized the necessity of having distinct and suitable priests to minister to the people in their own tongue. As early as the IV Lateran Council (1215), can. 9, the bishops were strictly commanded to provide priests suited for the work of administering to the people according to their own language and rite. These priests were not called pastors, nor was their status very clearly defined. There is no way of discovering whether they were to be attached to any one church exclusively.[16]

There has never been any general legislation commanding the establishment of national parishes. Consequently, it seems that the bishops were to use whatever means were most practical in supplying the care of the special needs of those who did not speak the common language of the place, according to the dictum of the Council of Trent that the people be cared for by territorial

[15] *Commentary,* VI, 509.

[16] "Quoniam in plerisque partibus infra eandem civitatem atque dioecesim permixti sunt populi diversarum linguarum, habentes sub una fide varios ritus et mores, districte praecipimus, ut pontifices huiusmodi civitatum sive dioecesum provideant viros idoneos, qui secundum diversitates rituum et linguarum divina illis officia celebrent et ecclesiastica sacramenta ministrent, instruendo eos verbo pariter et exemplo. . ."—c. 14, X, *de officio iudicis ordinarii,* I, 31.

parishes of their own, "or by some other useful method more adaptable to the local situation."[17]

In the United States where these national or lingual parishes are most numerous there has never been general legislation specifically ordering them. The Third Council of Baltimore vigorously urged that in the great seaboard cities, which were the melting pots of the multitudes of mixed immigrants, prudent priests who were familiar with European languages should be stationed to meet Catholic strangers and to assist and advise them.[18] More detailed plans for serving their spiritual needs were to be devised by the bishops according to local conditions.

Under the law of the Code bishops are incapable, without a special apostolic indult, of erecting parishes exclusively designated for the people of a particular foreign language or foreign nation, or parishes specifically restricted to certain families or persons. When the bishop thinks that parishes of those kinds are needed he should apply to the Holy See for an indult.[19] In instances where the language of the alien group in question is in no sense an official language of the nation, and where it is not commonly used by the other inhabitants of the territory, the application of the canon is clear.

A difficulty arose regarding the interpretation of the law in bi-lingual territory. When asked for a solution to the problem the Pontifical Commission replied that "in regions of mixed language, which politically form one civil state but in which more than one so-called official language is used, an apostolic indult is required for the erection of a parish exclusively destined for the faithful of a particular language, even if that language be one of the official ones and even if the parish to be erected have as its own a distinct part of the territory of the diocese."[20] The Code, as here interpreted by the response of the Commission, forbids the bishop on his own authority to establish language parishes in

[17] Sess. XXIV, *de ref.*, c. 13.

[18] III Plenary Council of Baltimore (1884), n. 234.

[19] Can. 216, § 4.

[20] Comm. Interp. Cod., Mai. 20, 1923—AAS, XVI (1924), 113.

any district where different nationalities are mixed. The response, however, apparently does not forbid him to do so in localities where practically the whole population employs one and the same language different from that of the nation, for in a case such as this there is really not a diversity of language in the district since all the inhabitants speak the same tongue, though it differs from the language more generally used throughout the country. This situation can be found in sections of the southwestern part of the United States, where Spanish is spoken almost exclusively. Consequently, in the latter case it seems lawful for him to do so without consulting the Holy See.[21]

For the bishop to alter the juridical status of an already established parish of this nature without first consulting the Holy See would be unlawful, but probably not invalid, because the invalidating phraseology of the first part of canon 216, § 4, is not extended to the second clause.

What has been said of parishes designated for the people of one language or nation applies equally to those designated for a particular group of persons or for a certain family.[22]

The need of special zeal for the spiritual welfare of the Negroes in the United States was recognized by the Councils of Baltimore. The Second Council left it to the judgment of each bishop to decide whether or not to found separate churches for them. It was thought unwise to issue a general decree probably because the work of caring for the newly liberated colored race was in a formative stage.[23]

By the time of the Third Council it was thought that the time was opportune for the widespread practice of establishing parishes for the Negroes. A mandatory note was injected into the legislation.[24]

[21] Coronata, *Institutiones,* I, n. 307, p. 353, footnote 3.

[22] Bishops were urged before the advent of the Code to strive to eliminate such family parishes. Cf. S. C. Episc. et Reg., Mai. 6, 1870—ASS, V (1869-1870), 638.

[23] II Plenary Council of Baltimore (1868), n. 485.

[24] III Plenary Council of Baltimore (1884), n. 238: ". . . decernimus ut Episcopi erectionem ecclesiarum, scholarum, domorum refugii pro orphanis ac pauperibus ad Nigrorum usum, ubi fieri poterit, omni nisu procurent."

Regarding parishes for the Indians nothing was decreed in any of the Plenary Councils of Baltimore. The Third Plenary Council established an episcopal commission "in general to promote the welfare of the Indians as the opportunity presents itself and by the best means at hand."[25]

It is possible that the problem of parishes for Negroes and Indians in the United States is one which, because of its local and more or less temporary nature, was left untouched by the compilers of the Code. These are certainly not family parishes. They can hardly be called personal in the limited sense in which that word is used in this place, because membership in them embraces a whole class of people, and is generic: whereas the personal type of parishes seems to embrace a more specific and individual membership. They are not based upon diversity of language, because frequently the vernacular is used.

Probably they can be included under the wording *pro diversitate nationis* which is general enough to include race. It is true that the wording of the Code seems to be primarily concerned with diversity of language when it deals with lingual and national parishes, but on the other hand it seems also to have intended to require an indult for all kinds except those that are solely territorial. The parity between lingual, national, and racial parishes is so natural that it would seem most reasonable to apply the rule: "*Ubi lex non distinguit nec nos distinguere debemus,*" and seek an indult in every case.

In deciding whether there is a commendable cause for seeking an indult for the founding of any of these kinds of parishes the bishop bases his judgment on whether the special type of parish is necessary and useful for the care of souls, and whether such care cannot be attended as well by the regular territorial parochial organization in which the vernacular of the place is used.

The request of the bishop for the indult is to be sent to the S. Congregation of the Council. It should contain an accurate

[25] N. 242.

and clear statement of the reasons why the special type of parish is desired and of the language that is to be spoken. It should also indicate whether the parish is bounded by any territorial limits within the diocese.

CONCLUSION

The welfare of souls, which always is the primary consideration in the matter of establishing parishes, is better safeguarded when the general law of the Church is most closely observed. Provision can be made for exceptional cases by the Holy See in individual instances. The following is a summary of the salient points in the procedure for the foundation of a new parish in the light of the conclusions presented in the body of this work.

If the territory assigned to the newly erected parish previously belonged to no parish, establishment is by the way of creation. If the territory assigned to the newly erected parish previously belonged to another parish establishment is by way of division.

Establishment by creation is mandatory wherever it has not yet been accomplished but in territory subject to the S. Congregation for the Propagation of the Faith it may be partially accomplished or entirely delayed until circumstances make the subdivision of the diocese, vicariate, or prefecture, feasible. Erection of new parishes by division is mandatory when certain other conditions are certainly realized; in doubtful cases it is left to the judgment of the bishop; otherwise it is forbidden.

The authority that is competent is the bishop or permanent administrator, and probably the administrator of a vacant diocese during the interregnum. The vicar general is not competent without a special mandate. In mission countries the vicar or prefect apostolic and the superior of the mission are competent. Local ordinaries cannot, without an apostolic indult, establish national, lingual, personal, or familial parishes. They are forbidden without an indult to introduce changes in the status of those which already exist. Although they are competent to divide all types of so-called religious parishes they cannot, without an apostolic indult, permanently incorporate new parishes with a religious institute even when the divided parish was itself incorporated.

The ordinary should conduct a local inspection either personally or through a delegate in order to discover whether a canonical cause for division is actually present, and to determine the location of the most satisfactory boundaries and other questions that may influence his decision.

No canonical cause is required for creation. The prime consideration is the good of souls and of the Catholic faith. A canonical cause is always necessary for valid division. Canonical causes are exclusively:

(1) Difficulty for a considerable number of parishioners to attend the old parish.

(2) Excessive number of parishioners in the old parish. Either cause, without the other, is sufficient. Cause is not present if without division the care of souls can be adequately provided by the appointment of assistant priests.

For the new parish there must be a sufficient population, consisting of at least ten families.

It is unlawful to erect a new parish by creation or division without obtaining the advice—not necessarily the consent—of those who are by law the advisers of the ordinary, namely, the cathedral chapter, the consultors, or the principal missionaries. Because of the doubtful interpretation of the law a bishop probably does not act invalidly if he decrees the founding of the new parish without holding the required consultation.

Clear and permanent boundaries are to be defined, or where that is impossible in mission countries, at least the principal Christian settlements should be designated.

Sufficient means of support are necessary for a valid foundation of a parish. They may be obtained from:

(1) Preferably a new endowment;

(2) The reliable contributions of the faithful, including stole fees if they are decreed as part of the endowment by the ordinary;

(3) The common property of canon 1500 which may sometimes supply an endowment;

(4) The endowment from revenue of the mother church;

(5) Any other certainly reliable source, but only whenever

the preceding forms of endowment are unobtainable or insufficient.

These various sources of income may constitute the means of support either singly or jointly.

Parishes should be erected by a formal decree of the local ordinary. This formal decree should be issued in a written document and should describe the boundaries, the site of the parish church, the endowment and other sources of income, and should declare whether the incumbent in the pastoral office will belong to the class of irremovable or removable pastors. The legislator prefers that the office be irremovable, and provides that the office of pastor of new parishes is by law irremovable unless the ordinary, after obtaining the advice of his consultors, decrees removability.

Provision should be made for a parish church and for a permanent residence for the pastor.

Aggrieved parties may have recourse to the Holy See, but only *in devolutivo*.

PARTICULAR CONCLUSIONS

1. Historically parishes are an example of legal practice that developed quite completely before general legislation took notice of it.

2. It cannot be concluded convincingly that the vicar capitular (or apostolic administrator) is not competent to found new parishes.

3. Consultation with the cathedral chapter (or consultors) and other interested parties is required for the lawful division of a parish. In practice the omission of this formality does not render a division invalid because there is legal doubt as to the interpretation of the law in this regard.

4. The endowment of the pastor's benefice should be distinct from the parochial patrimony, or common treasury, because the benefice and parish are distinct entities.

5. An indult is needed for the establishment of parishes for the Negroes and Indians in the United States.

APPENDIX

Formula erectionis novae paroeciae.[1]

Nos N. N., gratia Dei et auctoritate Apostolicae Sedis Episcopus N., omnibus praesentes litteras inspecturis salutem et in Domino benedictionem.

Inter praecipua Nostri pastoralis officii munera sane habetur commoda divini cultus pro omnibus singulisque fidelibus Nostrae curae commissis ita disponi ut unusquisque parochus cunctis officii per Nos ei attributi muneribus facilius satisfacere possit et valeat. Idcirco, prius auditis parochis incolisque paroeciarum . . . et Decano N. . . . et omnibus quorum interest, necnon etiam super tam grave negotium requisita Capituli Nostri Cathedralis (Consultorum Dioecesanorum) sententia per votum regulariter emissum, novam paroeciam ad divini cultus necessitatibus et religionis incremento plenius providendum canonice erigi decrevimus.

Quae quidem paroecia consistat intra limites infra dictas, scilicet.[2] ....
cum ecclesia paroeciali in loco N. . . . existente, et ad decanatum N. . . . spectet.

Nova paroecia erit inamovibilis (vel amovibilis) iuxta can. 454, § 3.

Dos beneficii parochialis in his temporalibus habeatur bonis, scilicet:[3] ....

[1] Adapted from Mothon, *Institutions Canoniques,* III, 211.

[2] Here should be described carefully, clearly, and in detail, the limits of the parochial territory in order to avoid future uncertainty and litigation.

[3] Here should be listed the temporal goods, movable and immovable, constituting the endowment of the benefice. If this endowment cannot be determined the local ordinary ought, in conformity with canon 1415, § 3, to declare at least in a summary fashion yet as definitely as possible, what source of income will provide for the expenses of worship in the parish and for the suitable livelihood of the sacred ministers.

Iura vero ac onera parochi pro tempore beneficiarii, praeter ea ex iure communi sunt et erunt, nempe:[4] ....

Quapropter, omnibus iuxta canones attente consideratis et mature perpensis, hanc dictam paroeciam N . . . ut supra descriptam, cum praefata ecclesia paroeciali in loco . . . sub titulo S . . . virtute praesentium canonice erigimus erectamque declaramus; cum omnibus iuribus, gratiis et facultatibus et fabricae consilio, quibus ceterae Nostrae dioecesis paroeciae, tam in spiritualibus quam in temporalibus, iuxta canones et statuta dioecesana frui et gaudere solent. In nomine Patris et Filii et Spiritus Sancti. Amen.

Datum N., sub signo sigilloque Nostris, ac cancellarii Nostri subscriptione, anno Domini millesimo nongentesimo . . . die . . . mensis . . .

N. N. Episcopus N.
N. N. Cancellarius.

Loc. † sigil.

[4] Here should be indicated the special obligations attached to the benefice in virtue of the foundation. If there are none the paragraph should be replaced by the following: *Iura vero ac onera parochi pro tempore beneficiarii sunt ea dumtaxat ex iure communi praescripta.*

BIBLIOGRAPHY

Sources

Acta Apostolicae Sedis (AAS), Romae, 1909- .

Acta Sanctae Sedis (ASS), 41 vols., Romae, 1865-1908.

Bruns, Herm. Theod., Canones Apostolorum et Conciliorum Saeculorum IV-VII, 2 vols., Berolini, 1839.

Bullarium Diplomatum et Privilegiorum Sanctorum Romanorum Pontificum, Taurinensis Editio, 24 vols., and appendix, Neapoli, 1857-1867.

Concilii Plenarii Baltimorensis II (1866) Acta et Decreta, Baltimorae: typis Joannes Murphy et Sociorum, 1868.

Concilii Plenarii Baltimorensis III (1884) Acta et Decreta, Baltimorae, typis Joannes Murphy et Sociorum, 1886.

Canones et Decreta Concilii Tridentini, ed. Richter-Schulte, Lipsiae, 1853.

Codex Iuris Canonici, Pii X Pontificis Maximi Iussu digestus, Benedicti Papae XV auctoritate promulgatus, Romae, 1918.

Codicis Iuris Canonici Fontes, cura Emi. Petri Card. Gasparri editi, 6 vols., Romae, 1922-1932, vol. 7, cura Emi Iustiniani Card. Seredi, Romae, 1935.

Collectanea S. Congregationis de Propaganda Fide, 2 vols., Romae, 1907.

Corpus Iuris Canonici, editio Lipsiensis Secunda post Aemilii Richteri curas . . . instruxit Aemilius Friedberg, 2 vols., Lipsiae, 1863.

Corpus Iuris Civilis, Institutiones—recognovit P. Krueger; *Digesta*—recognovit T. Mommsen et retractavit P. Krueger; *Codex Iustinianus*—recognovit et retractavit P. Krueger; *Novellae Constitutiones*—R. Schoell; opus Schoelli morte interceptum absolvit G. Kroll, Berolini 1928-1929.

Corpus Scriptorum Ecclesiasticorum Latinorum, editum consilio et impensis Academiae Litterarum Caesariae Vindobonensis *(Corpus Vindobonense),* Vindobonae, 1866-.

Harduin, Jean, *Acta Conciliorum et Epistolae Decretales ac Constitutiones Summorum Pontificum,* 12 vols, Parisiis, 1715.

Journel, M. J. Rouet de, *Enchiridion Patristicum,* Friburgi Brisgovae: Herder and Co., 1929.

Kirch, Conrad, *Enchiridion Fontium Historiae Ecclesiae Antiquae,* 2. ed., Friburgi Brisgovae, 1914.

Lightfoot, J. B., *The Apostolic Fathers*:
Part I, *St. Clement of Rome,* 2 vols., London: MacMillan Co., 1890;
Part II, *St. Ignatius and St. Polycarp,* 3 vols., London: MacMillan Co., 1899.

Mansi, J. D., *Sacrorum Conciliorum Nova et Amplissima Collectio,* 58 vols., Paris, Arnhem, Leipzig, 1901-1927.

Migne, P. J., *Patrologiae Cursus Completus*—Series Latina, 221 vols., (MPL), Parisiis, 1844-1855;—Series Graeca, 161 vols., (MPG), Parisiis, 1857-1866.

Monumenta Germaniae Historica (MGH), *Leges,* ed. Gregorius Pertz, 5 vols., Hanoverae, 1875-1889.

Nussi, Vincentius, *Conventiones de rebus ecclesiasticis inter S. Sedem et Civilem Potestatem,* Moguntiae, 1870.

Pallottini, Salvator, *Collectio Omnium Conclusionum et Resolutionum Congregationis Concilii ab anno 1564-1860,* 18 vols., Romae, 1868-1893.

S. Romanae Rotae Decisiones seu Sententiae, Romae, 1909-; *Decisiones coram Alexandro Falconerio,* 5 vols., Romae, 1727-1730; *Decisiones Recentiores,* 19 partes in 25 vols., Francofurti, Aurelianae, Romae, 1623-1703.

Schroeder, H. J., *Disciplinary Decrees of the General Councils: Text, Translation and Commentary,* St. Louis: B. Herder Book Co., 1937.

Thesaurus Resolutionum Sacrae Congregationis Concilii (Thes. Resol.), 167 vols., Romae, 1718-1908.

Works of Referfnce

Ayrinhac, H. A., *Constitution of the Church in the New Code of Canon Law,* New York: Blase Benziger, 1925.

—*Administrative Legislation in the New Code of Canon Law,* New York: Longmans, Green and Co., 1930.

(Bachofen), Charles Augustine, *The Canonical and Civil Status of Catholic Parishes in the United States,* St. Louis: B. Herder Book Co., 1926.

—*A Commentary on the New Code of Canon Law,* St. Louis: B. Herder Book Co., 1921-1929.

Barbosa, Augustinus, *Collectanea Doctorum in Concilium Tridentinum,* Lugduni, 1657;

—*Iuris Ecclesiastici Universi Libri Tres,* 3 vols., Lugduni, 1650.

Bastnagel, Clement V., *The Appointment of Parochial Adjutants and Assistants,* The Catholic University of America, Canon Law Studies, n. 58, Washington, 1930.

Berardi, Carolus Sebastianus, *Gratiani Canones Genuini ab Apocryphis discreti,* 4 vols., Venetiis, 1777.

Bingham, Joseph, *Antiquities of the Christian Church,* 2 vols., London, 1856.

Bouix, D., *Tractatus de Parocho,* Parisiis, 1855.

Bouscaren, T. Lincoln, *The Canon Law Digest,* Milwaukee: The Bruce Publishing Co., 2 vols., 1934 and 1937.

Brown, Brendan F., *The Canonical Juristic Personality with Special Reference to Its Status in the United States of America,* The Catholic University of America, Canon Law Studies, n. 38, Washington, 1927.

Catholic Encyclopedia, The, 17 vols., New York, 1907-1922.

Cicognani, Amlito, *Canon Law,* Philadelphia: The Dolphin Press, 1935.

Coady, John, *The Appointment of Pastors,* The Catholic University of America, Canon Law Studies, n. 52, Washington, 1929.

Conte a Coronata, M., *Institutiones Iuris Canonici,* 5 vols., Taurini: Marietti, 1928-1936.

Corradus, Pyrrhus, *Praxis Beneficiaria,* Venetiis, 1735.

De Luca, *Theatrum Veritatis et Iustitiae,* 16 vols., Coloniae Agrippinae, 1576.

De Meester, A., *Juris Canonici et Juris Canonico-civilis Compendium,* 3 vols., Brugis, 1921-1928.

Devoti, J., *Institutionum Canonicarum Libri IV,* 4 vols., Venetiis, 1827.

Doheny, William J., *Church Property: Modes of Acquisition,* The Catholic University of America, Canon Law Studies, n. 41, Washington, 1927.

Du Cange, Carolus Dufresne, *Glossarium ad Scriptores Mediae et Infimae Latinitatis,* 6 vols., Parisiis, 1733.

Duskie, John A., *The Canonical Status of the Orientals in the United States,* The Catholic University of America, Canon Law Studies, n. 48, Washington, 1928.

Fagnanus, Prosper, *Commentaria in Libros Decretalium,* 4 vols., Venetiis, 1697.

Fanfani, P. Ludovicus, *De Iure Parochorum ad Norman Codicis Iuris Canonici,* Romae: Marietti, 1924.

Feldhaus, Aloysius H., *Oratories,* The Catholic University of America, Canon Law Studies, n. 42, Washington, 1927.

Ferraris, F. Lucius, *Bibliotheca Canonica Iuridica Moralis Theologica nec non Ascetica Polemica Rubricistica Historica,* 8 vols., Romae, 1885-1892.

Ferreres, Ioannes B., *Institutiones Canonicae,* 2 vols., Barcinone, 1920.

Ferry, William A., *Stole Fees,* The Catholic University of America, Canon Law Studies, n. 59, Washington, 1930.

Godfrey, John A., *The Right of Patronage According to the Code of Canon Law,* The Catholic University of America, Canon Law Studies, n. 21, Washington, 1924.

Gonzales, Emanuel . . . Telez, *Commentaria Perpetua in Singulos Textus Quinque Librorum Decretalium,* 5 vols., Venetiis, 1899.

Hatch, Edwin, *The Organization of the Early Christian Churches,* London: Longmans, Green and Co., 1918.

Hinschius, Paulus, *Das Kirchenrecht der Katholiken und Protestanten in Deutschland*, 6 vols., Berlin, 1869-1897.

—*System des katholischen Kirchenrechts*, vol. II of the foregoing series.

Jaeger, Leo A., *The Administration of Vacant and Quasi-vacant Dioceses in the United States*, The Catholic University of America, Canon Law Studies, n. 81, Washington, 1932.

Kremer, Michael N., *Church Support in the United States*, The Catholic University of America, Canon Law Studies, n. 61, Washington, 1930.

Lesetre, H., *La Paroisse*, Paris, 1908.

Leurenius, Petrus, *Forum Beneficiale*, 2 vols., Venetiis, 1742.

Lotterius, Melchior, *De Re Beneficiaria*, Patavii, 1700.

Lydon, Patrick J., *Ready Answers in Canon Law*, New York, Benziger Brothers, 1934.

Maroto, Philippus, *Institutiones Iuris Canonici ad normam Novi Codicis*, 2 vols., Matriti, 1919.

Mothon, Joseph P., *Institutions Canoniques*, 3 vols., Paris, Bruges, 1922-1924.

Ojetti, Benedict, *Synopsis Rerum Moralium et Iuris Pontificii*, Romae, 1899.

Panormitanus, Abbas (Nicholaus de Tudescis), *Commentaria in quinque Libros Decretalium*, 8 vols, Venetiis, 1588.

Pirhing, Enricus, *Jus Canonicum in V Libros Decretalium distributum*, 5 vols., Venetiis, 1659-1677.

Pistocchi, Marius, *De Re Beneficiali*, Taurini, 1928.

Reiffenstuel, Anacletus, *Jus Canonicum Universum*, 7 vols., Parisiis, 1864-1870.

Rossi, Joseph, *De Paroecia*, Romae: Fredericus Pustet, 1923.

Schmalzgrueber, Franciscus, *Ius Ecclesiasticum Universum*, 12 vols, Romae, 1843.

Sebastianelli, Guilelmus, *Praelectiones Juris Canonici, De Rebus*, Romae: Fredericus Pustet, 1905.

Smith, S. B., *Elements of Ecclesiastical Law*, 9. ed., 3 vols., New York, 1887.

Smith and Cheetham, *Dictionary of Christian Antiquities*, 2 vols., London, 1876.

Thomassinus, Ludovicus, *Vetus et Nova Ecclesiae Disciplina*, 3 vols., Parisiis, 1688.

Van Espen, Z. B., *Ius Ecclesiasticum Universum*, 5 vols., Lovanii, Lugduni, 1778.

Vermeersch, A., Creusen, J., *Epitome Iuris Canonici*, 4.—5. ed., 3 vols., Mechliniae, 1931-1934.

Wernz, F. X., *Ius Decretalium*, 2. ed., 6 vols., Romae, 1906.

Wernz, Franciscus, Vidal, Petrus, *Ius Canonicum ad Codicis Normam Exactum*, 1. and 3. ed., 6 vols., Romae, 1928-1935.

PERIODICALS

American Ecclesiastical Review, Philadelphia, 1889-.
Apollinaris, Romae, 1928-.
Archiv für katholisches Kirchenrecht, vols. I-VI, Innsbruck, 1857-1861; vols. VII-, Maintz, 1862-. (AkKR)
Dublin Review, Dublin, 1836-.
Jus Pontificium, Romae, 1921-.
Periodica de Re Canonica et Morali, Brugis, 1905-; ab anno 1927: *Periodica de Re Canonica, Morali, Liturgica.*

BIOGRAPHICAL NOTE

Nicholas P. Connolly was born on August 14, 1909, at Oakland, California. He attended St. Joseph's Parochial School and St. Mary's High School, Berkeley, California. In 1925 he entered St. Joseph's Preparatory Seminary, Mountain View, California. After his course of studies made at St. Patrick's Major Seminary, Menlo Park, California, he was ordained to the priesthood, June 16, 1934. In the fall of 1935 he enrolled in the School of Canon Law at the Catholic University of America where he received the degrees of J. C. B. and J. C. L. in the years 1936 and 1937 respectively.

INDEX

CANON LAW STUDIES

1. Freriks, Rev. Celestine A., C.PP.S., J.C.D., Religious Congregations in Their External Relations, 121 pp., 1916.
2. Galliher, Rev. Daniel M., O.P., J.C.D., Canonical Elections, 117 pp., 1917.
3. Borkowski, Rev. Aurelius L., O.F.M., J.C.D., De Confraternitatibus Ecclesiasticis, 136 pp,, 1918.
4. Castillo, Rev. Cayo, J.C.D., Disertacion Historico-Canonica sobre la Potestad del Cabildo en Sede Vacante o Impedida del Vicario Capitular, 99 pp., 1919 (1918).
5. Kubelbeck, Rev. William J., S.T.B., J.C.D., The Sacred Pentitentiaria and Its Relations to Faculties of Ordinaries and Priests, 129 pp., 1918.
6. Petrovits, Rev. Joseph J.C., S.T.D., J.C.D., The New Church Law On Matrimony, X-461 pp., 1919.
7. Hickey, Rev. John J., S.T.B., J.C.D., Irregularities and Simple Impediments in the New Code of Canon Law, 100 pp., 1920.
8. Klekotka, Rev. Peter J., S.T.B., J.C.D., Diocesan Consultors, 179 pp, 1920.
9. Wanenmacher, Rev. Francis, J.C.D., The Evidence in Ecclesiastical Procedure Affecting the Marriage Bond, 1920 (Printed 1935).
10. Golden, Rev. Henry Francis, J.C.D., Parochial Benefices in the New Code, IV-119 pp., 1921 (Printed 1925).
11. Koudelka, Rev. Charles J., J.C.D., Pastors, Their Rights and Duties According to the New Code of Canon Law, 211 pp., 1921.
12. Melo, Rev. Antonius, O.F.M., J.C.D., De Exemptione Regularium, X-188 pp., 1921.
13. Schaaf, Rev. Valentine Theodore, O.F.M., S.T.B., J.C.D., The Cloister, X-180 pp., 1921.
14. Burke, Rev. Thomas Joseph, S.T.D., J.C.D., Competence in Ecclesiastical Tribunals, IV-117 pp., 1922.
15. Leech, Rev. George Leo, J.C.D., A Comparative Study of the Constitution, "Apostolicae Sedis" and the "Codex Juris Canonici", 179 pp., 1922.
16. Motry, Rev. Hubert Louis, S.T.D., J.C.D., Diocesan Faculties According to the Code of Canon Law, II-167 pp., 1922.
17. Murphy, Rev. George Lawrence, J.C.D., Delinquencies and Penalties in the Administration and Reception of the Sacraments, IV-121 pp., 1923.
18. O'Reilly, Rev. John Anthony, S.T.B., J.C.D., Ecclesiastical Sepulture in the New Code of Canon Law, II-129 pp., 1923.

19. Michalicka, Rev. Wenceslas Cyrill, O.S.B., J.C.D., Judicial Procedure in Dismissal of Clerical Exempt Religious, 107 pp., 1923.
20. Dargin, Rev. Edward Vincent, S.T.B., J.C.D., Reserved Cases According to the Code of Canon Law, IV-103, pp., 1924.
21. Godfrey, Rev. John A., S.T.B., J.C.D., The Right of Patronage According to the Code of Canon Law, 153 pp., 1924.
22. Hagedorn, Rev. Francis Edward, J.C.D., General Legislation on Indulgences, II-154 pp., 1924.
23. King, Rev. James Ignatius, J.C.D., The Administration of the Sacraments to Dying Non-Catholics, V-141 pp., 1924.
24. Winslow, Rev. Francis Joseph, A.F.M., J.C.D., Vicars and Prefects Apostolic, IV-149 pp., 1924.
25. Correa, Rev. Jose Servelion, S.T.L., J.C.D., La Potestad Legislativa de la Iglesia Catolica, IV-127 pp., 1925.
26. Dugan, Rev. Henry Francis, A.M., J.C.D., The Judiciary Department of the Diocesan Curia, 87 pp., 1925.
27. Keller, Rev. Charles Frederick, S.T.B., J.C.D., Mass Stipends, 167 pp., 1925.
28. Paschang, Rev. John Linus, J.C.D., The Sacramentals According to the Code of Canon Law, 129 pp., 1925.
29. Pointek, Rev. Cyrillus, O.F.M., S.T.B., J.C.D., De Indulto Exclaustrationis necnon Saecularizationis, XIII-289 pp., 1925.
30. Kearney, Rev. Richard Joseph, S.T.B., J.C.D., Sponsors at Baptism According to the Code of Canon Law, IV-127 pp., 1925.
31. Bartlett, Rev. Chester Joseph, A.M., LL.B., J.C.D., The Tenure of Parochial Property in the United States of America, V-108 pp., 1926.
32. Kilker, Rev. Adrian Jerome, J.C.D., Extreme Unction, V-425 pp., 1926.
33. McCormick, Rev. Robert Emmett, J.C.D., Confessors of Religious, VIII-266 pp., 1926.
34. Miller, Rev. Newton Thomas, J.C.D., Founded Masses According to the Code of Canon Law, VII-93 pp., 1926.
35. Roelker, Rev. Edward G., S.T.D., J.C.D., Principles of Privilege According to the Code of Canon Law, XI-166 pp., 1926.
36. Bakalarczyk, Rev. Richardus, M.I.C., J.U.D., De Novitiatu, VIII-208 pp., 1927.
37. Pizzuti, Rev. Lawrence, O.F.M., J.U.L., De Parochis Religiosis, 1927. (Not printed).
38. Bliley, Rev. Nicholas Martin, O.S.B., J.C.D., Altars According to the Code of Canon Law, XIX-132 pp., 1927.
39. Brown, Mr. Brendan Francis, A.B., LL.M., J.U.D., The Canonical Juristic Personality with Special Reference to Its Status in the United States of America, V-212 pp., 1927.

40. Cavanaugh, Rev. William Thomas, C.P., J.U.D., The Reservation of the Blessed Sacrament, VIII-101 pp., 1927.
41. Doheny, Rev. William J., C.S.C., A.B., J.U.D., Church Property: Modes of Acquisition, X-118 pp., 1927.
42. Feldhaus, Rev. Aloysius H., C.PP.S., J.C.D., Oratories, IX-141 pp., 1927.
43. Kelly, Rev. James Patrick, A.B., J.C.D., The Jurisdiction of the Simple Confessor, X-208 pp., 1927.
44. Neuberger, Rev. Nicholas J., J.C.D., Canon 6 or the Relation of the Codex Juris Canonici to the Preceding Legislation, V-95 pp., 1927.
45. O'Keefe, Rev. Gerald Michael, J.C.D., Matrimonial Dispensations, Powers of Bishops, Priests and Confessors, VIII-232 pp., 1927.
46. Quigley, Rev. Joseph A.M., A.B., J.C.B., Condemned Societies, 139 pp., 1927.
47. Zaplotnik, Rev. Johannes Leo, J.C.D., De Vicariis Foraneis, X-142 pp., 1927.
48. Duskie, Rev. John Aloysius, A.B., J.C.D., The Canonical Status of the Orientals in the United States, VIII-196 pp., 1928.
49. Hyland, Rev. Francis Edward, J.C.D., Excommunication, Its Nature, Historical Development and Effects, VIII-181 pp., 1928.
50. Reinmann, Rev. Gerald Joseph, O.M.C., J.C.D., The Third Order Secular of Saint Francis, 201 pp., 1928.
51. Schenk, Rev. Francis J., J.C.D., The Matrimonial Impediments of Mixed Religion and Disparity of Cult, XVI-318 pp., 1929.
52. Coady, Rev. John Joseph, S.T.D., J.U.D., A.M., The Appointment of Pastors, VIII-150 pp., 1929.
53. Kay, Rev. Thomas Henry, J.C.D., Competence in Matrimonial Procedure, VIII-164 pp., 1929.
54. Turner, Rev. Sidney Joseph, C.P., J.U.D., The Vow of Poverty, XLIX-217 pp., 1929.
55. Kearney, Rev. Raymond, A., A.B., S.T.D., J.C.D., The Principles of Delegation, VII-149 pp., 1929.
56. Conran, Rev. Edward James, A.B., J.C.D., The Interdict, V-163 pp., 1930.
57. O'Neil, Rev. William H., J.C.D., Papal Rescripts of Favor, VII-218 pp., 1930.
58. Bastnagel, Rev. Clement Vincent, J.U.D., The Appointment of Parochial Adjutants and Assistants, XV-257 pp., 1930.
59. Ferry, Rev. William A., A.B., J.C.D., Stole Fees, V-135 pp., 1930.
60. Costello, Rev. John Michael, A.B., J.C.D., Domicile and Quasi-domicile, VII-201 pp., 1930.
61. Kremer, Rev. Michael Nicholas, A.B., S.T.B., J.C.D., Church Support in the United States, VI-1930.

62. Angulo, Rev. Luis, C.M., J.C.D., Legislation de la Iglesia sobre la intencion en la application de la Santa Misa, VII-104 pp., 1931.
63. Frey, Rev. Wolfgang Norbert, O.S.B., A.B., J.C.D., The Act of Religious Profesion, VIII-174 pp., 1931.
64. Roberts, Rev. James Brendan, A.B., J.C.D., The Banns of Marriage, XIV-140 pp., 1931.
65. Ryder, Rev. Raymond Aloysius, A.B., J.C.D., Simony, IX-151 pp., 1931.
66. Campagna, Rev. Angelo, Ph.D., J.U.D., Il Vicario Generale del Vescovo, VII-205 pp., 1931.
67. Cox, Rev. Joseph Godfrey, A.B., J.C.D., The Administration of Seminaries, VI-124 pp., 1931.
68. Gregory, Rev. Donald J., J.U.D., The Pauline Privilege, XV-165 pp., 1931.
69. Donohue, Rev. John F., J.C.D., The Impediment of Crime, VII-110 pp., 1931.
70. Dooley, Rev. Eugene A., O.M.I., J.C.D., Church Law On Sacred Relics, IX-143 pp., 1931.
71. Orth, Rev. Raymond Clement, O.M.C., J.C.D., The Approbation of Religious Institutes, 171 pp., 1931.
72. Pernicone, Rev. Joseph M., A.B., J.C.D., The Ecclesiastical Prohibition of Books, XII-267 pp., 1932.
73. Clinton, Rev. Connell, A.B., J.C.D., The Paschal Precept, IX-108 pp., 1932.
74. Donnelly, Rev. Francis B., A.M., S.T.L., J.C.D., The Diocesan Synod, VIII-125 pp., 1932.
75. Torrente, Rev. Camilo, C.M.F., J.C.D., Las Processiones Sagradas, V-145 pp., 1932.
76. Murphy, Rev. Edwin J., C.PP.S., J.C.D., Suspension Ex Informata Conscientia, XI-122, pp., 1932.
77. Mackenzie, Rev. Eric F., A.M., S.T.L., J.C.D., The Delict of Hersey in its Commission Penalization, Absolution, VII-124 pp., 1932.
78. Lyons Rev. Avitus E., S.T.B., J.C.D., The Collegiate Tribunal of First Instance, XI-147 pp., 1932.
79. Connolly, Rev. Thomas A., J.C.D., Appeals, XI-195 pp., 1932.
80. Sangmeister, Rev. Joseph V., A.B., J.C.D., Force and Fear as Precluding Matrimonial Consent, V-211 pp., 1932.
81. Jaeger, Rev. Leo A., A.B., J.C.D., The Administration of Vacant and Quasi-vacant Episcopal Sees in the United States, IX-229 pp., 1932.
82. Rimlinger, Rev. Herbert T., J.C.D., Error Invalidating Matrimonial Consent, VII-79 pp., 1932.
83. Barrett, Rev. John D.M., S.S., J.C.D., A Comparative Study of the Third Plenary Council of Baltimore and the Code, IX-221 pp., 1932.

84. Carberry, Rev. John J., Ph.D., S.T.D., J.C.D., The Juridical Form of Marriage, X-177 pp., 1934.
85. Dolan, Rev. John L., A.B., J.C.D., The Defensor Vinculi, XII-157 pp., 1934.
86. Hannan, Rev. Jerome D., A.M., S.T.D., LL.B., J.C.D., The Canon Law of Wills, IX-517 pp., 1934.
87. Lemieux, Rev. Delisle A., A.M., J.C.D., The Sentence in Ecclesiastical Procedure, IX-131 pp., 1934.
88. O'Rourke, Rev. James J., A.B., J.C.D., Parish Registers, VII-109 pp., 1934.
89. Timlin, Rev. Bartholomew, O.F.M., A.M., J.C.D., Conditional Matrimonial Consent, X-381 pp., 1934.
90. Wahl, Rev. Francis X., A.B., J.C.D., The Matrimonial Impediments of Consanguinity and Affinity, VI-125 pp., 1934.
91. White, Rev. Robert J., A.B., LL.B., S.T.B., J.C.D., Canonical Ante-Nuptial Promises and the Civil Law, VI-152 pp., 1934.
92. Herrera, Rev. Antonio Parra, O.C.D., J.C.D., Legislation Ecclesiastica sobra el Ayuno y la Abstinencia, XI-191 pp., 1935.
93. Kennedy, Rev. Edwin J., J.C.D., The Sprecial Matrimonial Process in Cases of Evident Nullity, X-165 pp., 1935.
94. Manning, Rev. John J., A.B., J.C.D., Presumption of Law in Matrimonial Procedure, XI-111 pp., 1935.
95. Moeder, Rev. John M., J.C.D., The Proper Bishop for Ordination and Dismissorial Letters, VII-135 pp., 1935.
96. O'Mara, Rev. William A., A.B., J.C.D.,, Canonical Causes For Matrimonial Dispensations, IX-155 pp., 1935.
97. Reilly, Rev. Peter, J.C.D., Residence of Pastors, IX-81 pp., 1935.
98. Smith, Rev. Mariner T., O.P., S.T.Lr. J.C.D., The Penal Law For Religious, VII-169 pp., 1935.
99. Whalen, Rev. Donald W., A.M., J.C.D., The Value of Testimonial Evidence in Matrimonial Procedure, XIII-297 pp., 1935.
100. Cleary, Rev. Joseph F., J.C.D., Canonical Limitations on the Alienation of Church Property, VIII-141 pp., 1936.
101. Glynn, Rev. John C., J.C.D., The Promoter of Justice, XX-337 pp., 1936.
102. Brennan, Rev. James H., S.S., A.M., S.T.B., J.C.D., The Simple Convalidation of Marriage, VI-135 pp., 1937.
103. Brunini, Rev. Joseph Bernard, J.C.D., The Clerical Obligations of Canons, 139 and 142, X-121 pp., 1937.
104. Connor, Rev. Maurice, A.B., J.C.D., The Administrative Removal of Pastors, VIII-159 pp., 1937.
105. Guilfoyle, Rev. Merlin Joseph, J.C.D., Custom, XI-144 pp., 1937.
106. Hughes, Rev. James Austin, A.B., A.M., J.C.D., Witnesses in Criminal Trials of Clerics, IX-140 pp., 1937.

107. Jansen, Rev. Raymond J., A.B., S.T.L., J.C.D., Canonical Provisions for Catechetical Instruction, VII-153 pp., 1937.
108. Kealy, Rev. John James, A.B., J.C.D., The Introductory Libellus in Church Court Procedure, XI-121 pp., 1937.
109. McManus, Rev. James Edward, C.SS.R., J.C.D., The Administration of Temporal Goods in Religious Institutes, XVI-196 pp., 1937.
110. Moriarity, Rev. Eugene James, J.C.D., Oaths in Ecclesiastical Courts, X-115 pp., 1937.
111. Rainer, Rev. Eligius George, C.SS.R., J.C.D., Suspension of Clerics, XVII-249 pp., 1937.
112. Reilly, Rev. Thomas F., C.SS.R., J.C.D., Visitation of Religious, XI-195 pp., 1938.
113. Moriarty Rev. Francis E., C.SS.R., J.C.L., The Extraordinary Absolution from Censures.
114. Connolly, Rev. Nicholas P., J.C.L., The Canonical Erection of Parishes.
115. Donovan, Rev. James J., J.C.L., The Pastor's Obligation in Prenuptual Investigation.
116. Harrigan, Rev. Robert J., J.C.L., The Radical Sanation of Invalid Marriages.

www.ingramcontent.com/pod-product-compliance
Lightning Source LLC
LaVergne TN
LVHW050208080826
844660LV00012B/383